Anxiety is a F*#!@?, or is it?

© Copyright 2019 Sari
All content is original b
All rights reserved.

No part of this book may be reproduced either by mechanical, photographic, scanned or distributed in any printed or electronic form without permission.

Illustrations by ©Joe Rafiq, Instagram @the_drawlock

Cover and Book Design by Vicki Nicolson, Brand Creative
www.vickinicolson.com
For more information, visit: www.sarietaylor.com

DISCLAIMER: Although the author has made every effort to ensure that the information in this book was correct at press time, the author does not assume and hereby disclaim any liability to any party for any loss, damage or disruption caused by errors or omissions, whether such errors or omissions result from negligence, accident or any other cause. This book is not intended to substitute for the medical advice of physicians. The reader should consult a physician in matters relating to his/her health, and particularity with respect to any symptoms that may require diagnoses or medical attention. The methods described within this book are the author's personal interpretations. They are not intended to be a definitive set of instructions for this project.

I want to dedicate this book to my family, all of them.

My husband was with me throughout all of this. Through the difficult times, when neither of us had any clue of what was going on, or if it would ever end, he stood by me every step of the way. He still came to visit me daily in hospital, even after his bike wheel was stolen outside the private hospital!

My mum for being my cell mate. This will make sense as you read the book.

Bob & Stephanie Cooke for kindly writing the foreword for this book, as well as providing a safe and warm place for me to begin my journey training as a therapist and developing my understanding and awareness of what it means to be human.

Jacci Jones for being a wonderful friend and colleague, my partner in crime on this wonderful journey. Jacci also contributed a fantastic chapter in this book that I am sure you will love.

Nicola Bird for being the first person to introduce me to the principles in the most loving and authentic way.

My clients, every single one, who without them I wouldn't have been able to live my life with passion, and do a job I love every day.

My daughter, who has shown me so much about how to enjoy and embrace life, and makes me proud every day.

Foreword

Sarie has written her wonderful new book, "Anxiety is a F*#!@?, or is it?" charting her journey concerning anxiety, and where she has finally arrived.

Of course, we never really arrive anywhere; it's all part of our journey and transformation.

I have known Sarie for many years and she is a wonderfully creative, energetic, and "full of curiosity" person. This book shows her passion for helping people overcome anxiety, fears and panic in their everyday lives.

As well as Sarie sharing with you her own personal journey, difficulties and successes with "anxiety", she also talks throughout the book on how you can overcome anxiety within many areas of your life. Some of the areas she specifically talks about in this book are:

- Relationships
- Panic
- Pregnancy
- Low Mood

The title of this book, "Anxiety is a F*#!@?, or is it?" really sums up Sarie's personality, in terms of how we can all relate to the struggles and complexities of anxiety.

Sarie talks in this book about the '3 principles' originally shared by Sydney Banks, which have helped shift her perspective in how she sees and experiences anxiety. Her main motivation in writing the book is to offer a glimmer of hope to people dealing with anxiety, and for them to begin to see how anxiety can lose its power over them.

This book is accessible to the reader, and is written in a way that people will understand and identify with at a central level.

Sarie, as well as being someone who knows a lot about the subject of anxiety and how to deal with it in every day life, is also a qualified psychotherapist who spent four years understanding how people have become the way they are, and how to help people transform their lives and take charge of their own destiny.

Good Luck
Bob Cooke TSTA - Founder of the Manchester Institute for Psychotherapy UK

ABOUT THE AUTHOR

Sarie Taylor has had quite a varied career history, from working at Guinness, recruitment and sales, to then working in various probation and prison settings. Sarie then trained as a Transactional Psychotherapist for 4 years.

Sarie has worked in private practice for over ten years and has been running Coaching Healthy Minds for the last five years.

Sarie currently works and supports a number of organisations, educational settings, as well as writing books and manuals to support families across the world.

CONTENTS

1. Where it all started...

2. How best to read this book & Insights

3. Back to where it all started

4. I want to be a parent, but am I capable? Pregnancy

5. Panic attacks

6. Innate wellbeing – We are NOT broken

7. Relationships & Worrying about others

8. Mind, Thought & Consciousness with Jacci Jones

9. Trauma, Am I doomed?

10. It is what it is

11. Love

CHAPTER 1

Where it all started…

These words are written from my headspace at the time, a complete reflection of how I was then. You will see as you go through the book, that I wouldn't see this experience in the same light anymore, but I really wanted to share as authentically as I can, where I was at the time. However, I will also be sharing how differently I now see things too.

'Climbing the walls'. In that moment of complete fear and excruciating overwhelm, it dawned on me that this must be where the phrase climbing the walls came from. I moved from the bed, to the chair, to the floor, searching and searching for peace, wanting desperately for something to switch, and for this fear to subside. I have no idea what I thought moving from one piece of furniture to another would help with, but it just felt instinctive for some reason. I was going crazy. I was losing my mind and it was bloody scary as hell.

I sat in that room at my mum's house in my mid 20s, wracking my brain and torturing myself, as I just could not understand how I had ended up here. Not feeling able to leave my mums house, feeling fear that it's hard for me to even explain. I had travelled the world for goodness sake, what could have gone so wrong! It seemed to quickly escalate.

After a week, not only would I not leave the house, but the thought of my mum going out also filled me with complete dread. My mum also became a prisoner in her own home.

This is when I knew I had to do something, I just had no idea what, and the more I tried to figure it out, the worse I felt. The TV had become too loud and intense, even on the lowest numbers. A knock on the house door, maybe one of my five siblings, whom I love dearly, felt like it was enough to send me into a complete black hole of fear, that again I find really hard to explain. There are no words.

The thought of eating, and even smelling food made me want to run to the toilet and be sick. I was really ill, and felt like I was in a vicious cycle. The less I ate, the weaker I felt, and the more I would worry about being ill.

Ending up in hospital, I then embarked on a ten year plus journey of trying to fix myself, including training as a psychotherapist. I want to share this with you, and what I now know to be true about human nature, stress and anxiety, so that maybe your journey may not have to be quite so difficult or extreme. I will dip in and out of my history in this book, and then bring you back to now.

I want you to see that no matter what situation you currently find yourself in, there is always hope. I have had many people comment on my social media posts and blogs saying things like, 'you can't possibly have had bad anxiety if you think its that easy', 'you don't understand' and much more.

This was also part of the push to write this book as I see my experience as quite extreme and traumatic, and wanted to share how it all changed to the point where I am living my best life. It's not perfect but I don't need it to be.

In all honesty I have been threatening to write this book for over 10 years since my traumatic experience of anxiety and spending a month in The Priory. I know a lot of people would think I was lucky being in The Priory, its seen as a 'posh' or luxurious place to be. I just happened to have insurance through my work and so ended up in those four walls instead of four walls somewhere else.

Now I can promise you that it really didn't matter where I was at that time as I was lost in my head anyway, and everything looked bleak and depressing, even an expensive hospital. Actually, I believe the fact that I had health insurance, looking back, did me no favours, which I will talk about later on.

Since then I have trained as a psychotherapist, had years of therapy myself, as well as training in, and trying lots of other therapies such as NLP, hypnotherapy, EFT and reading 100's of self help books. Although there was an improvement in my ability to manage stress over the years, I still always feared the next time I would have the dreaded anxiety, and if I would ever end up back as bad as the first time. (Which never happened by the way, it was easier every time!)

Despite my own fears, I was able to get good results with clients, whilst sometimes needing to convince myself that I was OK, and good enough to help others. I questioned myself a lot.

It's often easier to support others, as we don't attach the same level of anxious thinking to their situation as we do our own. Unless you do find yourself doing that, then you may end up feeling like you have burnt out. In case I forget to mention this anywhere else in the book, if you are a professional working with others and suffer yourself, please do not allow yourself to believe you are not good enough to help others.

It doesn't mean you cannot support and help others. However, it is crucial that you allow yourself to be who you are, warts and all, and put yourself first.

Sitting here now putting pen to paper, I see that it was never the right time to write the book before, and that I was always meant to wait. It's only in recent years that I came across the 3 principles, originally described by Sydney Banks.

The 3 principles are Mind, Thought & Consciousness. I will not go in to explaining these like a textbook, as I do not want you to get bogged down in words and details. I want to just share my life experience of seeing these principles in my every day life, in the hope that you will see them more in your own. I know then that you will find peace of mind.

"Don't get attached to any words. They are only stepping stones, to be left behind as quickly as possible". Eckhart Tolle

It was when I came across these principles that I gained more clarity than I have ever had about my own struggles with anxiety, and as a result this completely changed my relationship with anxiety for the better.

Do I still get anxious?

Of course.

Does it stop me living my life?

Absolutely not.

I don't fear what I now see as a normal, natural human feeling anymore. In fact, I can safely say that I see it as a gift just like other feelings. It's a warning sign, a feeling that is valid and important, one I need to listen to, not run from. It keeps me alive! If you are thinking 'yeh right' – stick with me!

As I have started to explore with you already, there have been times in my life, like being stuck in that room at my mum's house, where if someone had said anxiety is a gift to me, I would probably have wanted to punch them! I am not a violent person but for that I would have made an exception.

At the very least I would have thought they were ignorant, didn't understand, and were very smug and annoying! I am not doing this to brag and say look how much easier and enjoyable my life is now. My intention is about giving hope to as many people as I possibly can, the kind of hope I would have died for when I was in hospital, yet couldn't find it anywhere!

This book is a way of me sharing with you exactly how I got to where I am now, so that it might inspire you to begin your own journey of discovery, with a glimmer of hope for the future. Let's get changing your relationship with anxiety!

CHAPTER 2

How best to read this book…

There is no right or wrong way to read this book. I may jump from one thing to another, as I am simply pouring things out of my head, and sharing them with you! This is a raw book, I am honest and open in everything I share, and I have purposefully not re-read it many times, as I didn't want to overthink what I was sharing, and just followed my gut instinct as I went.

It won't be perfect, but I just hope it's enough to at the very least get you exploring more! At the end of each chapter I will recap any insights that I had.

What do I mean by an insight?

Let's start with the dictionary definition as this is a habit I created from school when starting to explain anything! (I will talk more about habits later on)

'The capacity to gain an accurate and deep understanding of someone or something'...

If I was to simplify this even further, for me, the insights I have had along the way, although they can be life changing, have been often basic. They can be something that has been right in front of me all along but I couldn't see it for looking too hard!

Its simply just me seeing something differently to how I have seen it before, a shift in my perspective and as a result, given me some level of freedom I never knew existed.

For me insights are never ending. In fact, part of the reason I put this book off for so long, was that my insights were coming along and so the way I saw things was constantly evolving and changing. Until I had another insight, that it didn't matter that I kept seeing things differently, and that we will always evolve. I am sure in a year's time I will see some of what I talk about this book again in a different way, and that's perfectly OK.

I will often get asked by clients, how do I get insights and if I had to give you a few simple words I would say...

Be open-minded, explore as though you don't know anything. They will come.

CHAPTER 3

Back to where it all started...

So, as I have already said, I ended up in the hospital for a month. The exact amount of days that was available on my insurance (but don't get me started on that!). I remember the final day like it was yesterday, as it was the most lost and confused I have ever felt in my whole life. I was on three different sets of medication, two more than when I had arrived a month previously.

I had become comfortable in my surroundings, built up a false sense of security, and could not believe I was now being let loose to go on and live my life, or what I felt was left of it. I never believed it would be the same again, `I was now damaged goods.' (Spoiler alert – life has now never been better).

Now don't get me wrong, it wasn't all bad in hospital. In fact, some nights we all sat together and laughed so much it hurt. I met some amazing human beings in there, some lovely staff members and learnt to do a bit of yoga! My yoga career was fairly short lived though, as the lovely older lady who was helping me get more 'into' position, had stretched my legs that little bit further. This was so much so, that I let out an involuntary, but rather loud amount of wind, I was mortified. An already anxious Sarie suddenly wanted out of that room. I never went back. I have been to yoga classes since, but never quite reached my full potential, as I am still quite reluctant to stretch myself that bit further.

Back to my release.

I remember it was about an hour before my mum was due to collect me, and I was stood at the nurse's station asking for more Valium. For anyone who doesn't know what that is, it's a controlled drug that has a calming effect on the mind and body. I was almost begging for more because the idea of getting in the car and going home was unbearable but at the same time it was also all I wanted.

Mum arrived and suggested we go and grab a quick bite to eat before going home. The idea of that was great, but inside all I felt was sheer panic. I really wanted to prove I was OK and could manage. This was one of my strengths, or how I saw it at the time. Pretending to be OK.

Even other residents in the hospital used to comment on how OK I seemed, how quickly I had gone into the communal areas and chatted to people. It was habit, I was there, but I wasn't really 'there'. Habits can be easily formed. If we do something over and over it can easily become second nature, just like driving or brushing your teeth.

If you drive, it's unlikely that you have to tell yourself what to do to drive the car, you just drive. It's become habitual and often out of your awareness. We will then have thoughts about how we see ourselves in these habits, for example, I am a good driver or I am a nervous driver. These then become conditioned beliefs. They feel real as we think them often enough but they are not truth. They are a story, a habit.

I used to feel quite pleased at how people saw me, it fitted in with my idea of being strong and being a better person being able to show up and 'appear' OK. I didn't realise at the time that this was very much a part of my vicious cycle.

Back to the most effort I ever had to make just to order my lunch.

I remember suggesting that we just grab a sandwich and take it home. I walked into the shop grabbed what I wanted and walked up to the till and then it hit me again. How can I do this? I want to go back? I am not safe. All my senses were going crazy. My hearing went funny, I was in a bubble.

I was interacting with the lady at the till, but it was like I could hear the conversation, but I wasn't in it. I felt dizzy, weak and pretty much petrified, buying a sandwich! It passed. I made it out alive, and got home and that's where my long journey of exploration started.

At this time, I don't remember having any insights into what was going on. I was still desperately searching outside of myself, researching, asking others, looking for answers, seeing myself as broken and damaged, hoping for a miracle.

Where I am today, I look back and see where some of the difficulties lay for me, and how there was so much more for me to see, I just wasn't looking in the right direction. I now want to share some of that with you.

Insights...

Knowing what I now see to be true. We all have innate wellbeing. We all have the capacity to access peace of mind, listen to our gut instinct and follow our wisdom, which leads and guides us, always. Even in the hardest of times, we know what to do. Underneath that thought storm, excessive mind chatter, or whatever you want to call it, we have the capacity and resilience to tackle whatever comes along.

I have been asked by my clients many times, what do I mean by resilience. Let's get the dictionary out again...

Resilience
1. The capacity to recover quickly from difficulties; toughness
2. The ability of a substance or object to spring back into shape; elasticity

And that my wonderful fellow human beings, is a description of us in my eyes. Even when we can't see it, we are resilient in every sense if the word.

Having worked in this industry for some time now, I see how often we are looking in the wrong direction. By this I mean, that the minute we believe we are broken, mentally ill or unwell, as a society we can become fixated on labels and looking at what is wrong with us. How bad we are, how risky we are and how we need fixing.

What I want and hope for everyone is that we start to see as a society or for ourselves to see that we are innately well underneath. Take my time in the hospital for example. In the evening a room full of 'unwell' people sat laughing, loving and having fun connecting together, and at the time, it didn't seem like there was one 'unwell' person in there. How does that work?

I now see that as soon as my thinking fell away, I was connecting and enjoying myself, it was impossible for me to feel anxious at the same time. My innate wellbeing shone through at those times. Then as soon as the staff would arrive and say medication and bedtime, its like a switch would go off and I would feel like shit again.

The overthinking, anxious thoughts and the idea that I was broken and unwell hit me like a tonne of bricks again. What was different from the previous hour? Nothing, except my thoughts about myself.

I want to share a letter I wrote to the media on my social media accounts here. I wrote this because it's what I believe we really need to be sharing more, and I want you to hear it too.

A Letter to the world on Mental Health Awareness
C/o The media

I wanted to write an open letter about how I felt, and what I wish for all of us, in honour of Mental Health Awareness. I am a trained psychotherapist and an anxiety coach, but more importantly I suffered with severe anxiety, to the extent that I was hospitalised in my early 20's.

You could say we have come a long way in terms of attempting to end the stigma, talking more and welcoming change as a society. I see campaigns all over the media, which again is great as the media can reach SO many people all over the world. However, I can't help but express that I feel we are missing a huge opportunity.

These campaigns will often state facts and increase our awareness, and highlight to us what we are dealing with.

16 million people in the UK experience a mental illness

Suicide is the biggest killer of young people in the UK

I am sure we have all heard horrifying and quite frankly depressing and worrying statistics. Now again, awareness is a great start, but when we are in the throws of disappear, overwhelming anxiety or depression, in actual fact hearing these statistics and this level of awareness, without any answers, can increase the anxious thinking we already have.
It can add to the vicious cycle of worry and stress. In a lower state of mind, I may start to think...

What hope do I have?

It just is the way it is and I need to accept it, get on with it?

Yes, but what now?

As I sit here writing this now, I have just had Dermot O'Leary (the handsome chap that he is) give me another statistic and say that we need to talk more. Yes, talking is important. Talking can save lives.

Yet I also know that there will be countless people who have ended their lives that did talk. In fact, I know of two colleagues in my training institute alone, who had access to a whole host of therapist friends and colleagues, supervisors and trainers, who would have endless discussions about our mental health, that still went on to end their lives. Why?

I don't know for sure. What I do know, from my own experience with anxiety and depression, as well as the hundreds of people I have worked with and what they share with me, is that the key to reducing the overwhelm, and the feeling of being stuck with nowhere to go, is understanding how human nature works.

Understanding and increasing awareness of what is actually happening when we are in a panic. Knowing that feelings will pass, and this happens even quicker when we don't interfere with human nature by trying to figure it all out.

The key for me in changing me own relationship with anxiety was accepting who and where I was at that time. I also learnt to become more comfortable with the discomfort I was feeling and stopped trying to control absolutely everything. I started to see how resilient I was as a human being, even when I was anxious!

This is what I want everyone else to start to see but we need to be pointing them in the right direction and your campaigns could do this. Let's teach people about mental health. We are already? Actually, I think what you will find is that we spend a LOT of time talking about mental illness, diagnosis and it's not the same thing.

To give an example, I know there will be hundreds of thousands of people out there, as I once was, fearing the next panic attack. Wondering and avoiding situations, in an attempt to avoid the panic. This is exhausting and doesn't last; in fact, it can make us feel worse!

When I understood the basics about what is actually happening in our mind and bodies when we have a panic attack, it made such a huge difference to beginning of me breaking that fear cycle. That could be done in 90 seconds in an advert.

Rather than leaving people more aware of the crisis we feel we face, let's leave them with something they didn't know before, a new perspective on mental health, and a way forward.

So, to practice what I preach at the bottom of this letter, there is a link to some free resources to help you build your awareness and actually start the process of change instantly.

We can do this, all of us, with no exceptions.

I know I can't change the world and I am not famous so won't be able to access a huge audience, however together we can help educate each other one small step at a time. Let's support each other.

The key message for me, my biggest insight was that our thoughts create our feelings 100% of the time. No exceptions.

'Thought is not reality; yet it is through Thought that our realities are created'. Sydney Banks

Another insight I had over the years, was about the belief I had that it was good to show up and pretend I was OK. I worried a lot about the way I was affecting others. I will talk more about this in the relationship chapter. I didn't realise at the time that this was part of the cause, the resistance I had to being human, being me, and accepting who I was at any given time.

I now see that a large part of that fear was believing that I was now defined as this anxious person, and I didn't hold out much hope that I would ever be the same again. I now know that this is not the case. I know that diagnosis may have its place but for me it was very unhelpful at that time. I latched onto it and lived by it.

A client of mine that worked with me when I was a psychotherapist prior to exploring the 3 principles, who then joined me in exploring the principles, once thanked me for not giving her a diagnosis. This is the time in her life when she realised she was not her anxiety and never would be.

"A mental Health Diagnosis tells you WHERE someone is, not WHO they are". Dr Bill Pettit (One of my favourite mentors I have had the pleasure of exploring with).

With the amount of pressure I put on myself over the years to be OK, it was no wonder I got to the stage where something had to give. It's almost like playing a character, but not being able to switch off and go home and to be you. It's draining and unrealistic. Plus, think about the type of messages you could be sending to yourself.

You are not good enough so you need to pretend to be someone else.

You can't be vulnerable.

You are affecting others too much when you are like that.

Others are better than you.

You are different, weird, strange, odd, and not OK.

The list is endless. Imagine saying those things out loud to someone else. Not very nice is it? Yet we can do this to ourselves habitually for weeks, months or even years! In fact, imagine if someone said that to you. You probably wouldn't want to be around them much! Yet, you are implying these things potentially to yourself a LOT.

I was doing this a lot without even realising. In fact, if I were asked if I beat myself up, or criticised myself, I would have said no. I was a confident person; of course, I wouldn't do that. Once I started to see it, I then saw how much I was doing it, and how detrimental it was for me.

The other thing that I believe is important to highlight is the word in our vocabulary, which I believe is the most over used and unhelpful word EVER, and links in to a lot of what I have just said.

SHOULD

One of the most commonly used words I hear each week! I said in one of my coaching videos the other day that if we eliminated the word SHOULD from our vocabulary then most people's anxiety would drop massively, instantly!

Most people, who use this word A LOT, use it again out of habit to beat themselves up, set unrealistic expectations, and finally as a way to make themselves feel guilty for being inadequate!

The word SHOULD is a dangerous word when misused!

Dictionary definition of should:

Used to indicate obligation, duty or correctness, typically when criticising someone's actions.

Imagine using that word all day every day to keep yourself in check! Harsh isn't it?

This word is not a reflection of truth either, its purely a word to describe a belief or a collection of thoughts around what we see our obligation or duty to be, nothing more.

In actual fact we could eliminate this word and still survive, maybe even thrive! Try it…

The language we use day to day can have a significant impact on our expectations of our self and others. When I talk to people, particularly clients, it never surprises me the way they talk about themselves. Lots of 'I am like this', 'I have always been' and 'its just the way I am'. Yet adding a simple little extra two words on the end can change the whole meaning,

'Until now!'

Try adding that to your current stories. How does that feel?

'I have always been anxious' – What does always mean? Every second of every day, which will not be true. We often bulk experiences together, and then interpret them as the way we always are. Still not true.

'Until now', instead can again change the whole meaning and leave space for hope. That's all we need to remain open minded to allow insights to just come to us. In the past again I would have resisted saying 'until now' and if someone had tried to tell me I couldn't predict the future and that I could change my relationship with anxiety, I would use the words that rolled off the tongue,

'Yes BUT'.

Then I would come up with all the reasons and excuses as to why my experience couldn't and wouldn't change but not for the want of trying. Actually, allowing myself to eradicate the words 'yes BUT' was also very liberating. The past does not dictate the future, so 'yes but' is an illusion, prediction and no more guaranteed than anything that mystic Meg could tell you.

CHAPTER 4

I want to be a parent, but am I capable? Pregnancy.

If you are a male reading this title thinking this isn't for you, all about pregnancy and parenting, well it is. We all work in the same way psychologically, and insights are not about the content, more about the learnings that come from the experience, which we can all relate to. Men are parents too, and have also been parented in some form or other themselves.

Fast-forward a few years. A lot of therapy. A new career was starting, I was in the middle of my training as a psychotherapist (which if I am totally honest, I only started to fix myself. I knew I 'had' to have therapy to train, so I thought it would be a sneaky way of getting help without having to admit I was still struggling!)

I started to get a huge overwhelming urge, aged 28, to be a mum. However, I was petrified. Could someone with my mental health history become a mum? What if? What if? What if?

For the most part, I was able to see that I had progressed and that there were times where I felt more than capable to become a parent. Other times I didn't. I saw this at the time as me being inadequate. Why was I not consistently confident in my ability? I now know it's because I am human, and it's totally normal! My daughter was planned. We had discussed that it was what we both now wanted, but yet it was one evening after a party, a little bit tipsy, that we said sod it! Luckily, I must have been mega fertile, otherwise I may well have talked myself out of it again and again.

We fell pregnant very quickly, but I can remember right from the off with the research and what society implied, was that I would be likely to get postnatal depression. I was susceptible. What a way to get me started on the overthinking. That was a very real concern for me right from the beginning.

It wasn't all bad. My best friend also fell pregnant a few weeks before me, and it was wonderful. We were able to share it all together, from trying clothes on laughing at the size of our new boobs, to asking lots of, do you get this? Do you feel that? I was happy and managing better than I ever imagined.

Life happens and is out of our control.

I won't go into lots of detail, but when I was six months pregnant, my sister ended up in intensive care fighting for her life. A week into her intensive care stay, my dad was diagnosed with terminal cancer and given three months to live.

Welcome back anxiety.

I spent the next few months with such high levels of adrenaline, that I was constantly heaving and on the edge of throwing up. I didn't sleep very well, and I felt lost. I wanted to go and get the medication that I believed had been the only thing to keep me stable in the past. I didn't know any different. I knew it wouldn't be possible being pregnant, so I just carried on desperately trying to get through each day, worrying that I would lose my sister and my dad. My dad was a definite. I had never before experienced wanting time to pass quickly so I could get my baby out safely, but also wanting time to stand still so my dad would be here longer.

To cut a long story short. My sister was diagnosed with type 1 diabetes and thankfully managed to get well again, although her life would be forever changed. My dad lived longer than expected and sadly died when my daughter was approximately nine months old.

I actually managed to hold it all together, whatever that means! People had told me I 'was doing well'. At the time holding it together simply meant that I hadn't gone back on medication, and I hadn't ended up in hospital. These were my measurements, my way of checking whether I was on track or not, and yet these were the same things that I was completely fearful of, my route to failure!

Its funny how we create our own goal posts, our own perceptions, when actually anything that happens is OK. It has to be, we can't control it. This was also part of the problem for me, which I will explore in the insights and the end of this chapter.

Sadly, the inevitable happened, and my dad passed away peacefully at home with all of us around him, including my nine month old baby girl. Although he couldn't have asked anything more, and neither could we in terms of how to go when we have to, those final moments are still very difficult.

As you will know if you have lost a loved one, the next thing that happens is all the organising and preparing for the funeral. We often seem to find this strength and ability to get through, that we never knew we had. There is an insight in that too!

Just when I thought I couldn't feel any worse, the worst happened. I actually went to a slimming world meeting months later, I was delighted in that moment, as I had lost about 9lbs in the space of a week. It was also at this point that I realised, shit, there's only one other time I had lost that amount of weight so quickly, and I was on a slippery slope into a severe anxiety and depression episode.

Within the space of a week, I had to phone my husband at work and my mum, and ask them to get to me quickly as I couldn't be on my own for a minute longer. It had hit. Within another day, I was at the doctors getting some medication and crying none stop. My mum took my daughter to her house for a few days to give me a break. That was one of the most heartbreaking moments I can ever remember as a parent so far.

'What a shit mum was I that I needed her taking away from me?'

'How on earth could I not just pull myself together and look after her?'

'What if I could never get her back?'

'Maybe I should never have got pregnant in the first place, I should have known I wasn't capable'.

'My husband is going to hate me for this'.

'I have no choice; I can't look after myself even'.

'I hate myself'.

And this list goes on...

Obviously, my mum did an amazing job of taking care of my daughter, and I started to feel slightly more able to breathe after a short break. I then managed to go and stay at my mums with my baby and my mum, so that I could take care of her with my mum's support for a while.

I can remember that time so clearly as it was also my birthday that same week, and everyone was asking me what I wanted. I didn't want anything, nothing felt worthwhile. If anything, the fact that it was my birthday felt worse as the more I thought about what I should be doing. The more my thoughts went to what I SHOULD be doing, the worse I felt. There's the shitty cycle again!

In the end I asked for a Nintendo DS at the time, as I was able to distract myself playing the snake game for hours on end! A way of focusing my mind on that game rather than how awful I felt, but ultimately the thoughts would always creep back in, usually when I got to the more difficult levels on my game and I couldn't concentrate enough!

After a few weeks I was getting back on my feet, despite feeling like I had been hit by a bus, drained and again forever changed, I was getting there. Its interesting that as I tried to recall those times when I felt a bit better, there was nothing, a blank. I can tell you details about what I even had for tea when I was 'failing' and struggling, and yet when I was finding my feet, my memory didn't seem to see that as important to recall!

This is a habit that again we can form over time, focusing on the difficult and forgetting actually how wonderful and robust we are, and that we always get there in the end.

Insights...

Imagine if I was to ask my mum to have my daughter for a few days now because I wanted a break, holiday, work or simply time away. I wouldn't feel guilt at all. Why? Well I am human and I am my own person separate from my daughter, plus I know she is also OK with time away from me too. Yes, she is my priority and the most important person in my life. I am so much more able to be a better parent when I honour my own feelings too. After my mum has said yes, I would probably start to feel excited and look forward to the time that lay ahead the time for me, or me and my husband together. It's important.

Yet in the story I have just told, my mum had my daughter for a few days without me, and I felt like the worst person EVER. I was abandoning my baby. I was a terrible mother. I shouldn't have even been allowed to have a baby. What? What's the difference between the two situations? Why did I experience them both so differently? My own thoughts, my expectations and my judgements about myself. We are creating our reality 100% through our thinking, and mine was not always painting the best picture!

"Your thoughts are like the artist's brush. They create a personal picture of the reality you live in".

Sydney Banks

Here is a simple example of this that you will have already seen if you have my Healthy Mind Manual for Families.

Everything is inside out. I am talking about human nature and how we experience everything as a human being. What do I actually mean by that? Everything that

I talk about in this book, all the insights I share will all point back to this.

We experience every second, minute and hour of each day from the inside – our thoughts, our mind. Let me give you an example of what I mean.

Imagine you and a friend are walking in the park. A dog owner is walking their dog from the opposite direction, and as they reach you, they slow down and start to make conversation. You all have a brief talk for a few minutes and then the dog walker walks off. You and a friend then start to reflect and talk about the brief conversation. You both see things very differently.

You: Ah they were really nice and what a cute dog! Friend: Are you serious I thought they were so strange; I didn't like them at all!

Now you have both had the exact same conversation, with the exact same person, same place, same time and so on. Yet you both had a very different experience, one of you felt happy and the other felt uncomfortable, so how can that be if you are both doing the exact same thing? Now this may seem obvious, and you may well know the answer, but I will tell you below why I want to remind you.

You are both experiencing the conversation with the dog walker completely, 100% through your own thoughts. Your thoughts then create your feelings of happiness or discomfort for example. In some ways this is pretty obvious when you look at it like this. Your thoughts may differ depending on your past experience, and patterns or stories you have created in your thoughts.

For example, in this situation I have just described, your thoughts may have gone something like this:

You: I love dogs they are so cute, this person must be nice if they have such a nice dog that seems well looked after, it's polite to chat with those that make conversation, I really agree with what they are saying, I wish I had a dog, I might get one, and so on and so on.

You will have a lot of random thoughts in your head during the conversation, some of which you may even say out loud. These thoughts create feelings. Warm thoughts create warm feelings.

Friend: I feel a bit on edge around dogs, I wish this person hadn't stopped, I shouldn't really be talking to someone I don't know its a bit odd, I don't feel comfortable, I hope they don't talk for long, why is my friend asking so many questions about this dog?

These thoughts may create feelings of fear and frustration.

Now as I said, you may or may not have already known this. Yet even when people do seem to know that our thoughts create our feelings on an academic level, they can worry that its things outside of us that 'make' us feel a certain way. I hear it all the time. My partner makes me anxious. My job makes me anxious. It's only ever our anxious thoughts about something that creates feelings of anxiety.

So, in the example I have given, the friend may think that if he or she feels on edge after the conversation, that it was the dog walker that made them anxious. Yet if that were the case, both people having the conversation would feel the same, yet they felt very different about it. It was not the dog walker making anyone anxious; it was the friend's thoughts about the walker and the dog that made this an uncomfortable experience for them.

If we consider this example and look again at the thoughts I was having relentlessly when my mum took my daughter to give me space, its no wonder I felt awful.

A big difference now, that I could not see then, was that I was putting such huge expectations on myself, with all the bullshit thoughts I was having, and more to the point, believing!

At a time where I was vulnerable, dealing with loss and trying to find my feet with a great deal of change, I showed myself very little love and compassion. I criticised myself daily. I compared myself to everyone else and my head was a complete noisy whirlwind of worry. The way I see it now is that we can all fall down at times, its part of being human. Yet when we hit the floor, we can get up; we do get up. The way I was talking to myself, beating myself up was like me digging a huge hole.

Every comment, every thought was me digging a bigger and bigger hole. This hole was ready for when I fell. This meant I didn't fall and get back up. I had a hole to climb out of first, one I had dug through my thoughts.

"Life is like any other contact sport; you're gonna get your knocks. But it's not the knocks that count; it's how you handle them. If you handle them with anger, distrust, jealousy, hate, this in return is what you are going to get. But if you handle these knocks with love and understanding, they don't mean much. They just dissipate". Sydney Banks

I now see I was forever running from myself. Since my spell in the hospital, I feared ever returning and so as soon as I felt any discomfort or intense feelings of overwhelm it was the beginning of me feeling like I needed to fight myself to avoid the worst case scenario. I was trying too hard to be OK.

I was already OK; I would just talk myself out of it, riddled with anxious thoughts creating my anxious feelings. The more I resisted what was (accepting that I was human), and tried to avoid the discomfort of my feelings, the longer I remained stuck and afraid. I often ended up stuck in a cycle of fight or flight, which I will talk more about in the panic chapter.

"If the only thing people learned was not to be afraid of their experience, that alone would change the world." Sydney Banks

One of the analogies I use for this, is that trying to stop your thoughts when you are stuck in a cycle of overthinking or a thought storm, is a bit like being stood out in torrential rain and using a towel to dry yourself whilst the storm is still raging. I am pretty sure you would give up using a soaking wet towel to dry yourself, and just wait for the storm to pass, knowing and trusting that somehow you would dry eventually. It's the same with our thoughts, they do pass and there are better ones to come but we need to give up the idea that there is something we need 'to do' about the thoughts we are having.

CHAPTER 5

Panic attacks

Most of us, if not all of us will experience this in our life in one form or other. My experience was that once I had my first one, I was so in fear of the next that I lived in a cycle of worry about panic. In the media or on TV we will see the typical experience of hyperventilating or blowing into a brown paper bag and yet panic attacks can show up in many ways.

My experience of a panic attack was that I would get so overwhelmed so quickly that I would vomit. This would be the peak for me and then I would start to settle. The sheer boost of adrenaline in my body felt too much to process and I would be sick. It was almost then like the act of being sick would become my focus in that moment and my thinking would start to fall away.

We experience the beginning of a panic attack on a daily basis, if not more than once a day! Say for example, you are laid in bed and you hear a loud bang in another room. It's likely you will instantly think 'What's that?' You may feel instantly startled and tense; the adrenaline will start to kick in. Then you will very quickly have more thoughts about it such as, I need to go and see what it is. What if someone is in my house? Are my children ok?

Then your wisdom, gut, will tell you what to do. You may decide to get up and go and look. You may wake your partner up if they are asleep next to you and so on. All this time the thoughts would be racing and the body will be reacting physically too. You feel your heart pounding, you may feel sick.

You then walk into the hall to see that something has fallen and broken, smashed to the floor, which created the loud noise. You then see the cat looking sheepishly up at you! Instantly you know what has happened and so your thoughts about the situation change, you stop pumping adrenaline into your body and over time you settle and reset. We can have the beginning of a panic attack, being startled for many things, even a door slamming, your phone ring tone going off when you didn't expect it and so much more. It's all harmless and just the bodies response to being startled.

Going back to when I was in fight or flight, a state of panic for days and weeks on end, what was happening? Well I struggled to find reassurance and lived in a constant state of being startled, which I fed continuously. Always looking for answers and reasons and not finding any. I just didn't understand and that frightened me.

If I was sat I a doctors surgery and they said they needed to inject me with adrenaline but to expect to feel a bit dizzy, sickly and shaky and that after five minutes it would start to pass, then I would just get on with it without too much fear or questioning and eventually my body would settle.

However, when I was in constant fight or flight I was struggling and resisting to accept that this was somehow my bodies normal response to something. I struggled to believe that it would ever settle and so my overthinking about the panic and overwhelm then meant that I was continuously pumping adrenaline into my system over and over again. It became a vicious cycle.

One of the most simple and helpful things for me in terms of managing the feelings of panic, was to have more understanding of what was actually happening in my body and why.

Let me tell you a little bit about what happens in your brain when you stress and worry. The oldest part of our brain, the most primal and under developed part, often called the Lizard brain or Reptilian brain, is the part of the brain making sure you stay alive!

It is where the flight, fight or fear reactions are dealt with, and it also regulates body temperature, regulation of heart rate and so on. It's where we create patterns of behavior and habits, but it's not too concerned in long term solutions.

I see it a bit like the A & E department of the brain. When you go into A & E, they are there to keep you alive and deal with any immediate symptoms and issues – they don't treat any long-term issues, as they are really there to just keep us alive (just like your lizard brain).

This part of the brain is immediately responding to your messages that you may be in danger. This is great if we are faced with some kind of emergency and need to be prepared, but imagine when you are worrying about what may happen next week, next month or next year – you are sending a message to the lizard brain that you are in danger through your thoughts! The brain will then respond as though you are in immediate danger and react accordingly!

It doesn't have the ability to work out whether you are over reacting, overthinking or worrying about the what if's – it takes what you are telling it literally, and does exactly what it is meant to do!

It may speed up your heart rate – getting you ready to run or fight for example – yet when you are just sat watching TV and not planning to fight or run away from any danger, it can feel uncomfortable, and we then overthink that feeling of discomfort, again sending a further message of danger and so the cycle continues. I will be going on now to talk about those feelings of discomfort.

Sometimes when we feel stressed or anxious, we can get cross with our symptoms, but that's kind of like asking someone to do something really important for you, and then getting cross with them for doing it.

I hear people talking all the time about how they are going to fight their anxiety, face up to it and tackle it as though it's some kind of monster. I understand it can feel like that, I've been there many times, but it really isn't effective to try and fight anxiety.

This may sound like a very random example, but I am full of those! I see fighting anxiety similar to trying to kill yourself by holding your breath. You can't. Now when I first started to use this example I actually googled to see if it was possible, although my gut told me it wasn't. The furthest anyone has got by trying to hold their breath is that they passed out and when they did, their body instantly kicked back in and they started to breathe again.

This is the thing about our bodies, they are amazing and they work in favour of keeping us alive, we are survivors. The more we try and fight nature's way and the system our bodies have in place, the more frustrating and the more suffering we may experience.

The reason I wanted to explain what happens when we send messages of danger to our brains is because I want you to know and have peace of mind that your body has all of this covered. In the 3 principles this is covered when we talk about universal mind/wisdom. This will be explored in a chapter covering the 3 principles written by a wonderful friend of mine in Chapter 8.

We don't have to tell our heart to beat or our lungs to fill with air to breathe, it just happens. Thoughts are also taken care of in the sense that they come and they go, they always pass and new thoughts come. This process happens so much quicker and with more ease when we don't interfere with what is. I appreciate that the actual simplicity of this can seem difficult to get our heads around. I tried so hard, interfering with what is, to fix myself.

Again, going back to the example of when I was in hospital and at times was so engrossed in laughing and connecting with others, that the overthinking fell away and I felt like my old self. I saw this happening with so many of us in that room. We had stopped interfering with our natural way of being, we accepted ourselves. In that moment, we were present and just enjoying what was without expectation.

Insights...

Over a number of years, I have had countless insights about thoughts coming and going, and still do regularly. Sometimes we can get lost in our thinking and need a reminder, this is when we can see new things, new insights.

I want to share an extract from the Power Of Now, Eckhart Tolle

"Enlightenment: Rising above thought
Isn't thinking essential in order to survive in this world?

Your mind is an instrument, a tool. It is there to be used for a specific task, and when the task is completed, you lay it down. As it is, I would say about 80 to 90 percent of most people's thinking is not only repetitive and useless, but because of its dysfunctional and often negative nature, much of it is also harmful. Observe your mind and you will find this to be true. It causes a serious leakage of vital energy".

Eckhart then went on to say,

"This kind of compulsive thinking is actually an addiction. What characterises an addiction? Quite simply this: you no longer feel that you have the choice to stop. It seems stronger than you. It also gives you a false sense of pleasure, pleasure that invariably turns into pain".

I was definitely addicted to overthinking every little detail in my life. My lizard brain had come up with a way of making me believe I was in control by constantly planning for the what if's and evaluating what had been. A habit was definitely created and I felt stuck in it.

I even remember some days when I was so anxious, and then something would distract me, once I finished what I was doing, I would then sit and try and remember what I was anxious thinking about before. I would be thinking I hadn't figured it all out and had to go back to it to sort it!

I now see how much energy and value I was giving to my thoughts, I believed them to be true and putting such importance on figuring it all out in a desperate attempt to avoid hospitalisation again. I now see that it was doing this very thing that put me there in the first place.

Whilst I remember, let me tell you what I mean by bringing thoughts to life and giving them value. I am in Manchester and can remember very clearly when the MEN Arena bombing happened. Now we see on the news all too frequently that people have been bombed, usually in other countries. When I might see a banner pop up on the TV that says three people killed in a bombing in Syria.

Now I will have thoughts about that and those thoughts will create a feeling, a response to my thoughts about it. Yet without wanting to sound like I am not compassionate, those thoughts will pass and so will the feelings and I will continue with my day.

Now when I saw a snippet on the news about a bomb in Manchester, I brought that to life in my mind. I wasn't there and I didn't know anyone who was there (although I have worked with people who were there since), and yet it had a much bigger impact on me than seeing that there had been a bomb in Syria. Is that because I don't value a Syrian's life as much as someone in Manchester?

Absolutely not. It's because I started to research, I was sat on my phone looking up the events of the bombing as well as watching on the news with the volume turned up, full concentration and full energy given to thinking about the situation. The more I thought about it, the more intense my feelings were about it. I reacted to it in my thoughts as I was up the road. I pictured myself or my family being in that situation, yet I wasn't directly affected by the bomb in the same way I wasn't by a bomb in Syria.

If I was to then link this back to my experience of being in hospital with anxiety, which I found traumatic on a number of levels, every time I had a feeling of anxiety my thinking would take me back there.

What if I ended up back there?

What would it do to my family?

What if I was even worse this time?

All thoughts creating instant feelings of fear and frustration as well as a sadness, meaning I was experiencing that moment as though I was back there. I wasn't. I was experiencing my thinking in that moment, living in the feeling of those thoughts.

This was a huge place of resistance for me for many many years. The fear of 'what if'. One of the insights that changed this for me was realising that in actual fact I could never get a cast iron guarantee that I would

NEVER end up back in hospital. I was unable to predict the future and control the outcome.

I could try and avoid it, but ironically the harder I tried to avoid it; the more I would feel like I was going to end up back there. I then had a further insight into this, where something started to click when I realised that even if I did end up back there, I would survive, I would get through it.

This started to change the way I thought about it. I was not as panic stricken when it entered my mind, when I started to think about it, I could see a glimmer of hope even amongst the panic.

I didn't have to 'do anything' to see this. It came to me as if by magic (that's wisdom for you), the more I saw things from another perspective, the less the thoughts would crop up.
All I have 'done' if I had to be specific is explored the three principles and been very open minded to what I have heard and seen. Interestingly when writing this book, I have had more thoughts about my time in hospital as I am bringing it into my awareness, but they are not creating feelings of fear.

I have a knowing that it's hard to explain, that I will not end up back in that hospital, and that thought is quickly followed up with, and if I did, I would be OK. This is the end of the thought process; I know it's taken care of and it passes as quickly as it comes.

I heard a quote for the first time about the principles by Dr Bill Pettit, my wonderful mentor. I am not sure if it was originally his explanation, but he reminded me that the 3 principles are not a prescription, they are a description.

Basically, they are not a strategy, something we need to 'do' in order to get better. They are a description wonderfully brought into the mainstream by Sydney Banks and now so many other wonderful coaches. A description of human nature, our very being, and the way we work as humans. The more we see and understand the description, the truth of what it is, the less we keep searching for a prescription!

I can remember in the days where I was still trying really hard to fix myself and be OK, spending hours and hours of time not to mention the thousands of pounds I spent, I just wasn't able to see that it was much easier than I ever knew.

It's almost like when you hear a riddle and then when you get the answer it's so simple, and for a minute you will almost search for it to be wrong because it can't be that easy, and 'how did I not see it'. We didn't see it for looking. That's what was happening with me.

I had researched and tried so much to fix anxiety that I was massively over complicating it. I was attached to that over-complication in some ways because I needed to be able to justify all the hard work I had put into being anxious as well as trying to fix it.

The simplicity of all of this scared and frustrated me, it seemed too good to be true but then the more I would see, the less I could deny them truth that was showing up daily. Even in the simplest of ways. I can remember watching a programme with my husband.

It was about a child being abducted, who was eventually found dead. A lot of the experience of watching that for me was distressing and unnerving. I knew it wasn't a true story and that the characters were actors, but I felt uneasy.

Of course, I did. All the way through I just kept thinking about how I would ever cope in that situation. How would my daughter ever cope if that happened and some other pretty gruesome thoughts?

At one point my husband piped up with something like. They've messed up there, she didn't have those shoes on in the first part of that scene, now they are different. I remember my reaction was to think what a dickhead. Does he not realise how I am feeling right now and is that all he cares about? I then laughed to myself

57

because I realised that he was simply having a different experience to me because his thinking was different.

Neither of us was right or wrong. Just two different experiences of the same thing. I know that if I had not seen this, I could have then gone down a road of believing I couldn't watch stuff like that as it affected me too much. That's not true. There were many different ways I could have experienced that programme. This is also similar to how phobias develop.

My mum has a phobia of frogs for example. It's nothing at all to do with the frog otherwise we would all be afraid of frogs and we are not. What causes the discomfort in the phobia is all the layers of thoughts.

Take the words, 'frogs are slimy'. This is neutral and means nothing. However, if my mum then starts to alter that, take the idea of them being all slimy, 'what if they jump and I feel them, I feel sick just thinking about it, now I feel hot and faint' and so on. Mum then may feel that the only way to avoid this discomfort is to avoid the frogs. Poor frogs it's not their fault they are slimy!

I hope you get the gist. You are only ever experiencing the feeling of your thoughts. They will always change and pass.

CHAPTER 6

Innate wellbeing – We are NOT broken

Back to the days where I was at a complete loss as to how to fix myself. I now know that none of us are broken and that we all have access to our innate wellbeing at any time but I haven't always seen it like this.

One of the big things that was missing for me when I was stuck in a cycle, habit, addiction, whatever you would like to call it, I lost all faith and trust in myself to be OK. I felt doomed.

I felt destined to spend my whole life fighting and doing everything I could to be OK. Completely missing the point all along, that I was already OK. I just didn't see it that way.

Believe me I wanted to; I hadn't taken the easy way out; fighting against yourself is one of the most draining experiences ever. In fact, I would go as far to say that its soul destroying. Again, how I saw it then.
I now know that it was just how it had to be for me to be where I am now and although I would have much preferred a direct route to where I am, it wasn't to be and I accept that now.

Again, I am not trying to be smug or annoying here and that you may be reading this book now from a perspective where I was a while ago. Yet I can't help but share how I see it now, even with the risks of irritating and frustrating people, I am here to share the truth and show you some light at the end of the tunnel no matter how you choose to interpret that right now.

I remember exploring these principles and feeling jealous of those that seemed to be much quicker and better at 'getting it' than me. I now see that they were no less or more capable than me, they were just at their own place in their own journey and no matter how much I wanted it to, this would not affect or speed up my own process.

I now love the fact that we are all equal as I am forever learning and having more insights from everyone around me, my clients included. I am not working with clients to help them get 'better' like me. I am not working with them to 'show' them how to improve their life.

I am simply alongside them in their journey, sharing what I have seen and continue to see to be true for me, whilst they have their own insights in their own time.

Back to when what I am sharing with you now, would have sounded to me like bullshit. It didn't have a beginning, middle and an end, and so I wasn't interested. I wanted a prescription, a strategy, and a quick fix. I had lost trust in my guilt instinct, I couldn't hear it. All I could ever hear when I was listening to myself was panic.

I am always encouraging people to listen to their gut rather than their panic thoughts, and I am then more often than not asked the same question. How do I know the difference?

I could never explain it as eloquently and simply as George Pransky does here…

"Wisdom is always playing like a soft flute in the background. But when a brass band is playing (our typical conditioned thinking) you can't hear the flute. The flute never stops, but it can only be heard when the brass band stops. The brass band is always going to take a break, even for a moment. That's when the flute can be heard".

So, you may or may not have heard of words like, wisdom, gut instinct and innate wellness. Think of it as your own internal guide or sat nav. It can be our ability to know right from wrong. It's what gets us through difficult situations. It's our innate wellbeing, that we were born with, and ALWAYS have access to.

It's a constant knowing, and ability to just know what to do. When people come to me in times of stress or anxiety, its often as though they don't believe they have this guide. It's as though they stop knowing what to do, and don't seem to trust or see that they are well. They often feel they are broken or about to break.

Imagine the sun is shining bright (just like your innate wellness) and then all of a sudden clouds appear (thoughts). Then it starts to rain (even more thoughts), and it starts to seem much darker, almost as though the sun has disappeared. Well actually we know it hasn't just disappeared, but that it's just covered, or doesn't seem the same, because there are other things in the way, maybe a storm?

We can also have thought storms too, and it can seem like our shine or sunshine (innate wellness) has gone. It hasn't. It's still there somewhere for us to access at any moment.

We are surrounded by stories and situations, even in our own life, where we just show up and face difficulties with a strength or determination we never knew we had! It's very common for people to say to me that they are OK in a crisis but it's the little things that stress them out.

Their wisdom guides them in these situations. And at the times they feel they can't cope, they are listening to the drums and the flute appears as though it's stopped, it hasn't.

I know that when I was highly anxious, although my wisdom, my innate wellbeing showed up regularly, it's like I dismissed it and hunted for the anxious thoughts again. I think my habit of looking for a fix and some sort of perfection, I sometimes felt like my wisdom wasn't enough so I would keep searching. This would obviously create a whole load of more anxious thoughts and low and behold I felt anxious. I now know that my wisdom, internal guide, is doing it's best for me in any given moment and I can always rely on it.

I once did a presentation about the three principles with a group of people where a wonderful mother asked a question openly in the group, as she was worried for her children.

I can't remember the specific details, but I still think it's a great example of our wisdom at play. The family ended up in a horrendous situation where the father had a gun pointed at him in a robbery in front of the rest of the family.

Thankfully he was OK and came out of the situation alive. The mothers concern was for the longer-term consequences of this for her children (I think it was two girls). This mum was asking me in a nutshell if she should be worried about one more than the other and is there anything she should be doing.

This wonderfully brave woman then went on to explain that as the intruder left, one of her daughters froze and just did not move. The other started to collect all of her belongings that she saw of any importance to trade with her as she fled the home.

These are two very real and touching examples of fight or flight in action. Was one child dealing with that situation better than the other? Absolutely not.

They were both reacting in a way that felt right for them. They followed their internal guidance and survived it. Yes, it would have been extremely distressing and overwhelming, but they coped and they managed. Their wisdom and inner guide carried them through.

In these kinds of situations, it would then be very easy to go over with the children how awful it must have been and how they felt. (Which if they want to do is absolutely OK and important that we listen)

However, it's also very important that these children see that in that moment they just knew what to do that felt right for them and that they always have access to that guide no matter where or when.

Insights...

I realised the importance and freedom that comes from seeing this in action, and to hear stories as well as experience my own wisdom in action, see my own innate wellbeing like I mentioned previously. (Laughing in hospital)

It was important because it gave me freedom. Freedom not to plan for every eventuality and possibility that could ever be! I am pretty sure that family never expected to be in that situation that evening, although they may well have worried about lots of alternative ones that never happened.

I don't expect myself to never get caught up in the noise of the drums, I am human. However, when I do, and I realise, I give myself permission not to have it all figured out. Phew, what a relief. Just on a side note, how do I realise when I am caught up in it?

Usually because I feel crap. I feel anxious or angry or sad or fed up. As I know that those thoughts don't come from nowhere, I can see that I have a whole load of thinking going on and so allow myself to take a step back from having it all figured out.

I realised that instead of feeling like I was going to die, that actually panic attacks were safe. It was just my body's response to what I was telling it! I was OK – phew!

I also realised that fighting this was pointless, tiring and keeping me stuck! I didn't need to fight anymore.

CHAPTER 7

Relationships & Worrying about others

When I suffered severely with anxiety, I often had difficulty in relationships. Not just with others, but also with myself! The ironic thing is, that although my relationships became difficult, others may not have even known, it was mainly in my own head and perception, stories I created and really believed to be true. I would still torture myself with it.

As I have already said, the man I am now married to, Matt was with me as my boyfriend when I ended up being hospitalised, and every episode since then.

When my anxiety would spiral, my ideas about who I was in the relationship would alter drastically. I would go from believing I was a good enough catch, to believing...

There was no way someone would stay with me.

I would never find anyone else either. I would have imaginary conversations in my head about how I would let a new person (once my boyfriend had left me) know how bad I was, and what they were letting themselves in for.

I would often come to the conclusion that I would date them, and then once anxiety reared its ugly head, I would just disappear without a trace! I am laughing to myself reading this thinking that when Matt reads this, he will probably be unaware of how many imaginary dates I have been on behind his back, as a result of all the times I decided he was going to leave me, when in actual fact he was doing his best to support me.

I have no doubt at times he has considered leaving me, it happens to most people. It's also something we have discussed.
It's just thoughts, and when not acted upon, its meaningless and perfectly OK. Again, often in relationships we want to control, and know categorically that they will not leave us, and always

treat us the best they can. I will cover this again in the insights.

The irony of this common thought pattern at times of anxiety, was that it was such a waste of time and suffering, as I am now 20 years into a very positive and loving relationship. It's not been perfect for either of us, but it's perfect in its imperfections. No further dates were required. I wish I had a crystal ball at the time; maybe I would have given myself a break!

We are always experiencing our relationships through our thinking because actually there are no exceptions to us experiencing anything in life without thought. This may seem like it could be a good and a bad thing at times. It can be a bad thing and cause suffering, if like me you are able to take a row about not putting the bins out, to me searching Google for a new flat that I was moving in to, within the space of 20 minutes! All in my head.

When I was exploring how all of this stuff works, human nature and the three principles, one of the first times I really saw that my relationship was also experienced through my thinking was one night at about 1am lay in bed.

Matt is an accountant and he will often have to work later at the end of each month. It's the only career he has ever had in all the time I have known him, so it's never been any different.

Despite the fact that Matt would usually work late at the end of the month, I could experience this in such different ways. Same people, same situation and so on. I had experienced feeling annoyed, upset and frustrated, maybe even angry at times that we hadn't seen much of him, and yet again I would be off to bed on my own whilst he sat in front of the computer.

Then the following month I would offer him a drink, offer to keep him company and experience real love and appreciation for how hard he worked for us as a family.

So, two very different experiences and set of feelings, completely and utterly experienced through my thoughts at the time.

Like me in the example I have given we can shift from having extremely low tolerance for others to the other end of the scale where we experience them through love and compassion.

I sometimes laugh at myself now as I find myself getting caught up in the negative thoughts. When this happens, I literally tell myself I need to put my compassionate glasses on and will even ask myself directly, if I was to view this situation through my compassionate eyes what might I see?

"A couple looks at their differences and feels bad about their marriage. It is not the differences that make them feel bad. It is the negative feeling that accompanies the act of looking at those differences. The practice of analysis, self-doubt and fault finding muddies your view and makes frogs out of princes". The Relationship Handbook By George S. Pransky.

The likeliness is that I was in a lower state of mind the day that I was angry and so was holding on to negative thoughts, wondering, asking why and trying to figure everything out! When we are in a lower state of mind, it's not ideal for us to try and figure everything out, to wonder and question. Even Einstein told us that…

"We cannot solve our problems with the same thinking we used when we created them". Albert Einstein

Sounds easy doesn't it, just leave things be when you are in a lower state of mind?
Yet I struggled with this for years. I had created a habit of having to know and understand everything, to feel in control. Plus, my stubborn nature (again through my thinking around – why should they etc.) would keep me questioning everything and everyone around me. I needed to know and yet what I didn't realise at the time is that I would never know anyway!

Before I go on to talk about families and friends, I just wanted to mention intimacy. Now I won't embarrass my family by giving any details, but I do think it's important to mention that being anxious for a lot of people, can affect their sex drive. There is also another aspect to this where it has been implied that medication can affect sex drive, but I am not talking about that, as I am not medically trained so I don't know.

What I do know though, is that I did not want to be intimate when I was anxious, this worked in the same way as a lot of things I didn't want to do when I was anxious. It was because I was so focused on my anxiety, my head was so busy, and it was as though I didn't have time to even give headspace to anything else. This was a complete myth.

We don't need headspace to just be and connect with people. I would talk myself out of so many things, by checking in with my anxiety to see if I felt I was able, capable and had the headspace.

Then the cycle goes on. I would then tell myself I can't even do x, y or z. This would reaffirm that I wasn't good enough, and that anxiety was the biggest focus in my life, and that I had no choice about that. It was exhausting. I waited for the day when I would look forward to just saying yes to things without any ifs and buts. That day just never seemed to come. The more I wanted it, the further away it seemed to become.

I often get messages from those who have loved ones with anxiety, wondering how best to support them. I wanted to touch upon this as I appreciate it can be a really difficult thing to navigate. There are a few things I want to say.

You can't make someone worse – Often people will message me in a panic as they want to support their loved ones, colleagues and friends, yet they don't want to make the situation worse.

We all think differently and therefore we will all experience our own anxiety in our own way. This means there is no set answer. What I do know though, is that when we are closer to love and compassion, connecting with others in this way doesn't leave much room for worry and overthinking.

Rather than trying to find a solution for your loved one, or pushing them to do certain things that you think will help. Just ensure they know you are there and that they are loved. Just be alongside them with compassion. Accept them for where they are at that moment.

I appreciate that this can be frustrating and maybe even feel like you are not doing enough. They will also be frustrated and may even been looking to you for the answers, but the change only ever comes from the inside out.

I remember during one of my episodes (weeks of panic and anxiety that meant I stopped being able to function in my everyday tasks) I was crying uncontrollably telling my mum and my sister that I couldn't go on like this. I was expressing what was running through my head at the time. I didn't have an answer, I was exhausted and completely at a loss.

I wasn't suicidal, or my experience of feeling suicidal, in that I never ever actually wanted to kill myself. However, what I did want, is a way out of this excruciating overwhelm that I really didn't believe that I could cope with any longer. I wanted to go asleep and not wake up to how I was at that moment. I did however want to live, just not that way. Yet I couldn't find any answers.

As you can probably gather, I was really quite desperate for something to change and I was looking outside of me for all the answers, and had done for years. I can remember at one point my mum and sister suggested that they contact the crisis team (a solution in their eyes, or at least a suggestion) and yet to me it felt like another knock.

My immediate thought was what the f*&% are they going to do for me, I am likely to be even more qualified than they are, and I felt that I knew they didn't have the answers either. I also then went on internally to overthink the fact that my family must have thought I was really bad, a danger to myself and a lost cause with that suggestion. I absolutely know that not to be true.

They were nothing but supportive, caring and loving but equally at times I am sure they too felt desperate, scared and overwhelmed with how they could help or fix me. The reason I am telling you this is because this in itself can be a vicious cycle.

As I have already said, the best thing you can do is put your compassionate glasses on, tell them you love them and ask them what their gut instinct is telling them they need. You can make suggestions but then follow it up with the idea that these are all options and suggestions but actually it's important that they follow their gut instinct.

Back to what I was saying about relationships...

Disclaimer about relationships: I think it's really important for me to say that just because we are experiencing everything from the inside out, so it's always our perception we are experiencing, that doesn't mean we would put up with an abusive relationship.

It doesn't make someone's horrible behavior and treatment become our fault. Your wisdom and gut instinct will tell you if you need or want to leave, we just need to listen to it, and we can't hear it clearly when we are lost in overwhelming thoughts. Focus on you and you will find a way.

Insights…

Thankfully, I don't need to suffer in my relationship anymore, I just allow myself to feel angry or frustrated, happy and excited, and I am much more able to look at my marriage compassionately, and know we are both doing our best in any given moment. Don't tell Matt though!

Another insight I had over the years was that me saying 'no' was also a habit. Exploring my habits meant I could see that in actual fact, I could just as easily say yes!

Saying yes or no to something in advance actually has no direct link or correlation to how we will feel at the time. We can't predict the future and how we might feel and guess what? We are allowed to change our minds at anytime.

Once we label ourselves as anxious, we often feel that we must consult with our anxiety, as to whether we can do something or not. That's kind of like consulting with an imaginary friend. It's not a 'thing'. It's a feeling created by thought in any given moment.

I know historically I gave it so much power over my decision making. I would often tell white lies about why I couldn't do things. I didn't want people to know the truth. My truth at the time, yet I now know the truth is, that I was a human being, putting far too much pressure on myself to be perfect.

It affected my friendships and relationships.

When I felt stuck in this cycle, I would go one of two ways. I would cry and beg my boyfriend to please stick by me and I would promise to 'sort myself out'.

The next day I might tell him to leave as there was no point, and that he would go anyway, he was only with me out of pity.
I would again have imaginary conversations with myself about how I didn't need anyone, and was better off on my own.

I wasn't, I was just scared that the decision of whether I was in or out of a relationship was out of my control.

You will see from my insights that I didn't need to think any of this.

I will share some of the conversations or realisations that my husband and I have had, now that we are much more able to communicate and share how we truly feel, without fear of upsetting or judgment.

I won't share too much detail as this is not a book written by choice for my husband, but hopefully will share enough that you may have insights into your own relationship with others when anxious.

In the days of severe anxiety, Matt (my boyfriend and now husband - we've been together just over 20 years now) did what he knew best. He was, and still is a very practical person. Every time I started to hide away, literally in my bed, he would 'do' everything that needed doing in the house.

He would be very busy sorting everything as well as working. This may sound great and really helpful, and in some ways it was; yet I would overthink this often as the beginning of him trying to end it. Him avoiding me, telling me it was over.

A huge insight I had into relationships was that they are never in our control.

All the stories I created were me often trying to be in control, when I couldn't. As I have said, I know now actually to a degree he was avoiding me; we have talked about it. He was avoiding me because he was scared for me and had no idea what to do to help. Looking back now I have no idea how I expected him to because I had no bloody idea either!

I was then able to start to see that I am a good enough catch even when anxious! If it's meant to be it's meant to be, I can't control it and worrying about creates more anxious thoughts, and guess what...more anxiety!

CHAPTER 8

Mind, Thought & Consciousness with Jacci Jones

I feel like I've known Sarie all my life, the reality is it's been about eight or nine years, she's kind of the Ying to my Yang. We've been alongside each other through lots of life events over those eight or nine years. So, when Sarie asked me to contribute to her book it was both a privilege and honour that she thought of me.

I first met Sarie when I was facilitating some training she attended on behaviour management, we hit it off straightaway. Behaviour management was kind of my thing back then, I was a foster carer and was looking outside of the box for ways to help the teenage boys we were caring for at the time.

It was Sarie who got me into Transactional Analysis Psychotherapy. We trained at the same Institute in Manchester, only I was a few years after her. And I suppose we both found 'The Three Principles' around the same time. Training to be a psychotherapist for me was another way of helping people, that was the reason I was doing it, not for any personal reasons after all, I didn't need therapy (little did I know).

My philosophy on life was 'suck it up buttercup and get on with it'. I'm not sure if you know that part of psychotherapy training in this country is that you are obliged to have weekly personal therapy as part of the training.

My theory of not needing therapy went out the window. I suppose I found out some things about myself, but to be honest I'm one of those people who doesn't like revisiting the past. If it wasn't that good first time round why would I want to go back and do it all again in a room with a therapist?

I think this is why 'The Three Principles' got me hooked from the start; it doesn't matter about your past, your experiences, your family or how you were parented. In fact, when I see clients now, I don't need to know anything about their history. Our past doesn't define who we are; often it's our thoughts about the past that keep us stuck.

So, what are 'The Three Principles'?

One of the things hopefully you will come to realise when reading this is that no matter what I write it will only ever be my thoughts and my reality about the understanding.

What is a principle?
Gravity is a principle. I'm not sure I've ever questioned what gravity is, I just know if I drop something it falls. So, I suppose my personal opinion of a principle is something that I accept without questioning on a daily basis. One of my favourite sayings is 'it is what it is, until it's not'.

My understanding around 'The Three Principles' is ever evolving so I will try to explain it from the place I am today, I have no doubt tomorrow it will be slightly different but that's okay.

'The Three Principles' are made up of Universal Mind, Universal Consciousness and Universal Thought; these three things were brought together by Sydney Banks a Scottish welder, in the 1970's. Although very clever in his own right he wasn't always seen that way in certain circles because his education was sometimes seen as inferior.

Universal Mind.

Universal Mind is constant and unchangeable, people explain it differently again what follows is my understanding.

It's a universal system that keeps everything running. Depending on your beliefs it could be your god or mother nature, it's a force or energy that has no beginning or end, it's neutral and it does what it does without bias or for the good of any individual entity.

It's how the sun knows when to rise, the leaves know when to grow and when to fall and probably how are we all came into being.

Basically, it's the be all and end all.

Michael Neill was one of the first people I came across when learning about 'The Three Principles' he has a wonderful way of explaining the unexplainable and this is what he says about Universal Mind

"The Principle of Mind: There is an energy and intelligence behind life. This is ever present but is not 'in control' – it has no inherent morality or apparent point of view. It simply ensures that but for the interference of external circumstance, acorns become oak trees, cuts heal, and life begets life".

If all that sounds a bit 'woo woo' and hurting your brain a little, the way I sometimes explain it to people is that it is kind of like electricity for a television. It's just there running in the background doing its thing, so the tele can be on, off, change channels, brightness, volume control, access the Internet and all the wonderful things smart TVs can do, without having to keep checking it can still do it.

Everything is interconnected and works in unison like a perfect symphony, no one thing is more important than another but together they create anything and everything.

It's funny that as I'm writing this and trying to explain something that I've never really thought so deeply about, I'm a little concerned, and it's took me right back to where I started. It's a principle. The more we attach words to it and try to explain it, the further away from the understanding it becomes, a bit like trying to catch water with a sieve.

So maybe it's just a knowing, that in the end, if we don't interfere Universal Mind will just continue to do its thing in the background without drawing attention to itself.

Universal Consciousness

One of the definitions of conscious is being aware of something, so Universal Consciousness relates to our awareness of how things work for us as human beings.

Personally I'm not sure our brains have evolved at the same pace as technology. To a certain extent they still function the way they did when we were cavemen and this can be a bit of a hindrance in the 21st-century, but again if we don't interfere and let things be, underneath all the stress and worry of modern day living, we are okay.

When I was first introduced to ' The Three Principles' I researched online and studied as much information from as many different sources as I could find, that's just how I am.

My awareness of how things work using 'The Three Principles' ebbed and flowed. One minute I thought I understood it and the next I thought I'd lost it. The harder I tried to learn the less I seem to understand and that again is one of the ways 'The Three Principles' work.

It's a knowing and a feeling that happens when you least expect it, it's an insight.

Have you ever had one of those moments when you've been struggling with something for what seems like an eternity and suddenly the answer comes to you as clear as day, when you stop pursuing something and it just happens? 'The Three Principles' is all about insight, and it's something you can't teach.

One definition of an insight is stated as "the capacity to gain an accurate and deep understanding of someone or something".

We all have the capacity to gain this understanding, in fact in my opinion we all do it anyway, but it is out of our awareness. That was a bit deep for me to get my head round when I first started exploring 'The Three Principles', and if you take anything away from reading this chapter; that would be my gift to you, to just explore, be curious, be human.

Another little gem from Michael Neill on this is: "The Principle of Consciousness: The capacity to be aware and experience life is innate in human beings. It is a universal phenomenon. Our level of awareness in any given moment determines the quality of our experience".

So, if we are all already have Universal Consciousness why do we need to learn about 'The Three Principles?

That's a really good question. Again, the answers I give come from my own personal exploration, because we often find ourselves stressed, worried and overwhelmed, our innate well-being and awareness can become clouded by overwhelming thoughts and feelings.

Part of this understanding is just knowing that underneath everything is as it should be. I often talk with clients about something Michael Neill spoke about. That no matter what the weather is like the sun is always in the sky. We don't question that, in fact we don't pay much attention to it.

It can be foggy, snowing, raining, a sandstorm or tornado, but out there somewhere there is the sun. It's kind of like saying our innate wellness is always there even when we are experiencing stress, worry or a thought storm.

The other thing worth mentioning when we talk about Universal Consciousness, awareness and our understanding is our 'State of Mind'.

Our state of mind is transient and fluctuates on a moment-to-moment basis. One moment we can be on top of the world, and the next have a feeling of impending doom. That's often what we do as human beings, we wait for the bubble to burst.

Going back to what I said earlier about our brain not developing and that often we still function as cavemen. A little bit of a sideline here bear with me!

In the good old days when there were Sabre-toothed tigers, and we had just invented the wheel, we needed to focus on the negatives for our survival. If our environment changed we needed to be aware of it so we could protect ourselves, and it worked because we are still here! It's always easier somehow for us to focus on the negative, and I believe that's because we haven't developed at the same rate as the world around us.

We can often react in the same way as a life-and-death situation, when we have forgotten to answer an email or a text message. Our brains can't differentiate between the two and that for me is where Universal Consciousness and our awareness can help us the most.

Our 'State of Mind' affects our awareness without a shadow of a doubt. When my state of mind is in a good place, I refer to that as 'Genius Jacci'. Everything seems to fall into place without much effort, I can throw negative thoughts and feelings off and life seems wonderful. However, when my state of mind is in the 'not so good place', at the bottom of the ladder so to speak, everything changes!

My negative thoughts stick around a lot longer, that then affects the way I feel, that then affects the decisions I make. (See formula at the end of this chapter). My awareness of how things work has packed its bags and gone!

I call this 'Numpty Jacci'. The awareness comes into knowing which one we are when we are in it. Making decisions as 'Numpty Jacci' is not the best idea, and usually there is not a good outcome. Whereas 'Genius Jacci' nails it every time. That's not to say she never gets it wrong but if she does, she doesn't beat you up over it. Whereas 'Numpty Jacci' can sometimes get it right, but will still put a negative twist on it. Funny how that works!

This is where the understanding of 'The Three Principles' comes together for me. So, we've looked at Universal Mind, that pretty much left to its own devices does its thing, so that's the electricity or the power behind us all.

Universal Consciousness is like the smart TV; sometimes it just does its own thing depending on what you were watching last time, (where your 'State of Mind' was). It can make suggestions going off where you were the last time it was on.

Kind of like what Facebook does when you Google support knickers, everything on your newsfeed is about supporting all your wobbly bits (sorry is that just me? Shared a bit too much information there).

Universal. Thought
The final part of the jigsaw is Universal Thought.

Here's Michael Neill again
"The Principle of Thought: We create our individual experience of reality via the vehicle of thought. Thought is the missing link between the formless world of pure potentiality and the created world of form".

Don't worry if you have to read that a few times or it doesn't make sense even after you've read it 10 times, that still happens to me!

Here's my take on Universal Thought.

Thoughts are neutral until we give them energy, and the energy we give depends on our state of mind and our awareness, (see it's all coming together).

So, if Universal Mind is the electricity or power and Universal Consciousness is the smart TV then Universal Thought is the programme we put on to watch.

Google says we have up to 60,000 thoughts a day. If we gave energy to all 60,000 thoughts, our heads would probably explode, and we definitely wouldn't have time for anything else. So, what we tend to do is give energy to the ones that mean something to us at any given moment.

Remember our 'State of Mind'? We often make a story up around the thoughts that we have, just like a television programme. If I'm 'Genius Jacci', the story will be a bestseller and everything works out well in the end, BUT……… if I'm 'Numpty Jacci' it's likely to be a whole 12 part series of mega disasters!

Unfortunately, we have no control over the thoughts that pop into our head at any given moment, but we do have control over which ones we give energy to. Which links into our consciousness and awareness and our 'State of Mind'. Sometimes it's like being on automatic pilot, thoughts are transient and neutral and just pass through if we let them.

As this book is about anxiety, I'll give an example of how this might work.

I don't consider myself to be an anxious person but as everyone does, I have moments where I feel apprehensive and nervous; having a whole range of feelings and emotions comes with being a human being.

Sometimes life can throw us a curveball that can affect our state of mind, if our Universal Consciousness and awareness kicks in, we know the system and how it works. If on the other hand our awareness is low, the negative, overwhelming thoughts can get hold and before we know it, we're stuck in a cycle.

I suffered from postnatal depression with all three of my children and it got progressively worse. My last child was born in November 2004. On Boxing Day of that year there was a massive tsunami in Indonesia. Now admittedly, due to postnatal depression my state of mind had taken a hit, and my thoughts went into overdrive.

At its worst point I wanted to move house to higher ground in case there was a tsunami near me, I really lost the plot. Every waking moment I felt anxious, one of the things I now know is that there is always a thought before a feeling.

As Sydney Banks creator of 'The Three Principles' says, "Your thoughts are like the artist's brush. They create a personal picture of the reality you live in."

And mine were creating the worst reality I could imagine. I was a foster carer at the time and refused to talk openly about what was going on for me, my thoughts were telling me that if anyone knew they would remove the children in our care.

So, I struggled on. Looking back I'm not sure at what point things changed but they did thankfully.

An interesting thing that I will always remember is that I was in the throws of a massive panic attack, when the phone rang. It was somebody calling about PPI. The thoughts and the massive panic instantly disappeared when I heard the phone ring.

Why was that?

Why is it possible for us to drop thoughts instantly when something else gets our attention? Along with the thoughts, the feelings disappear as well. That's our innate wellness. We all have it, we're born with it and we never lose it, it's like this sun, it's always in the sky even when the weather covers it and we can't see it.

'The Three Principles' is all about being human. There's a few equations that might help you move forward.

Thoughts = Feelings
Thoughts + Feelings = Actions

So, if we use that equation

Anxious thinking = Anxious feelings
Anxious thinking + Anxious feelings = Your Story
(whatever that may be)

To finish off here's a blog I wrote about putting a post on my business page.

My understanding of being human is always evolving and that's okay with me. When I take the pressure off and trust that my innate wellbeing or internal satnav will guide me, everything just seems much easier.

There's ALWAYS a thought before a feeling!
We humans, it seems, have anywhere from 12,000 to 60,000 thoughts per day.

Thoughts like 'mmmmm chocolate' come and go with not much impact but what about the thoughts we have that stick around a bit longer. Thoughts like 'what if I get anxious', 'last time I did that I made a fool of myself'.

These kinds of thoughts can prevent us from living the life we want; the reality is they are just the same as the mundane thoughts we have each and every moment the difference is we build a story around them.

Here's what I mean…

When I started writing this post, I was keen as mustard and raring to go, then the thoughts started. Here's how it went,

I'll put this post on my page
It needs to be an interesting, useful post
I'll have to be funny, no professional, no interesting?
What do I need to do to keep them reading it?
Oh crap, I don't know what to put now
What will get their attention and keep them reading?
Does it need to be educational?
I always do this, overthink then get nothing done
Oh FFS
Sod it I'll just post a meme

So, did I post a meme, NO. I wrote this, and if you're still reading something is familiar or pricked your interest.

If we don't notice the thoughts, we can create a whole story around them, and it becomes real. We create a feeling to go with the thoughts (usually a crappy one) then we act on those feelings, not doing something or doing something we regret later.
We can't stop our thoughts, it's part of being human, we can't stop our feelings either but we don't always need to act on them. We can just notice them and let the crappy ones go. They are like buses there will be another one soon enough and if it's a better one, hop on it.

Big Hugs
Jacci x

CHAPTER 9

Trauma, am I doomed?

One of the most common questions I get asked is whether trauma, or our past in general, means that we can't heal or change our lives. In short, the answer is NO.

Now it's important that I say before I carry on that at no point in this chapter do I want to discount people's experiences? I know that people experience some horrific situations in their lives. Some of the stories I have heard over the years would be enough to make you lose faith in humanity altogether. However, we can't change the past and I am pretty sure that whoever you are and whatever your history, you wouldn't want to continue suffering in your future.

Let me tell you a little about my history. I won't go into lots of detail as it's not necessary, but I thought it would be good to share so I can explain further what I mean by, not suffering in the future.

I am one of five siblings. We all grew up as a very close family, a big extended family with loads of cousins as my mum was also part of a big family growing up, and we all lived quite locally to each other.

Although I fought a lot with my sister growing up and my brothers irritated the life out of me, except for my baby brother who was born when I hit my teen years so I just saw him as a real life doll and loved taking him out. (He has since made up for the annoying stakes, as he got older though!) Despite a very normal amount of sibling rivalry, we were all very close. The type of close where we would fight and argue, but if someone outside of us five would say anything harmful, or threaten us in any way, we would all be there instantly for each other.

I was the oldest and always felt that I should be responsible in some way for the others. I still do to a degree but definitely not in the same way I used to. That's not because I don't care anymore, it's because I realised it's not my place and it was causing me unnecessary distress and worry.

I can remember being quite young and going through every person in my family in my head and literally asking myself, 'Are they OK?

Is there anything I need to do to make sure they are OK?' At one stage this would be nightly that I would do this. Nobody was asking me to, I just created a habit of doing it. It was my way of allowing myself to settle. Although as you can imagine if there was anything going on, which in families it always does, this could take quite some time!

The funny thing about habits is that in some ways our mind thinks it is helping us. It thinks it is leading us to do what we need to do to settle because at some time we decided it was helpful. Like any habit we do it enough times we start to have a belief that it's absolutely necessary.

I could give you a number of times and reasons this started with me but in actual fact I will never really know exactly how it formed. I will share a couple of examples with you though so I can explore with you what I mean.

My dad, who as you know sadly passed away over ten years ago, was in some ways the most wonderful, funny, caring, intelligent, compassionate and charismatic man you could ever meet.

I am not just saying that because he's no longer with us, he really was. He was also an alcoholic, who made some seriously shit choices over the years.
Shit choices where he put alcohol before his family, many many times. Too many times. This was the focus of a lot of my worries and overthinking as a child. It's important for me to say though that this was still a habit I created to try and make sense of things and keep my head above water.

As I said I won't go into all the details but those of you who have watched someone close to you with an addiction will know what I am talking about.

I say this because in all of this, in all of our worry and stress, it can be very empowering to see that I created the feelings from the thoughts about how my dad was or wasn't. Now you may read this and think well it was his fault. Yes, his shit choices were his fault, yet if I had understood at a much younger age how not to overthink and take an unhealthy approach to feeling responsible for everyone, it wouldn't have affected me in the same way. (This is why I am so passionate about children understanding this from a young age!)

How can me seeing that be empowering? Well it means I am not damaged, broken or doomed to be a victim of my experiences through life, there is always a different way and a freedom that comes with this understanding.

We are not our experiences; we simply feel them through our thinking at the time. I know for a while when I was anxious, I was looking for reasons. I think the reason I was looking is because if I could figure out exactly why I was anxious, maybe I could fix it.

I didn't realise at the time that although it may increase my awareness and give me a chance to talk through some things, it was never going to rid me of anxiety. Understanding how my thinking creates the feelings and then how I was continuously bringing that into my present world was what I needed to see.

I know there may be some people reading this and thinking she didn't go through that much and I am under no illusions that there were a great deal of people out there experiencing much more distressing situations than me, but this still all works in the same way.

Let me give you a more specific experience I had when I was in secondary school, that I recognise as a time when I went into overthinking overdrive. I really reinforced my ever-growing habit.

Not intentionally of course. It never is, it's a very innocent misunderstanding about how human nature works that can keep us searching and looking for ways to escape, we just don't realise what it is we are

needing to escape, that it's our own thoughts and judgment of ourselves.
That's where the endless suffering lies.

The school I went to was a school where people came from all over to go to. This meant that friends would be scattered all over the northwest, which made popping to each other's houses difficult sometimes. However, the plus side to this was that we did a lot more sleepovers, even on school nights! One of my best friends (I am lucky to have a few), who is still holding that wonderful title still now, lived on the other side of Manchester. I would say by the time we were in the second year, we were regulars in the week sleeping over at each other's houses.

This then progressed to holidays abroad with each other's families too. We became like sisters. I felt like her family were my extended family, and I think she felt the same way too. We had the some of the best times I can ever remember. We used to go to Tenerife twice a year sometimes, to the same place, and my friend came most of the time too.

We would see the same people every year, make the best friends, and we would be so upset when it was time to leave. The first thing I would do when I got home is to be on computer or teletext looking for the next holiday that I could convince my dad to book. (My dad never drank when we were on holiday, as mum would never have agreed to go otherwise, so this was also a time of fondness for us as a family).

I was then invited to go to Lanzarote with my friend and her mum and dad. Of course, I jumped at the chance. It started off as wonderful as our usual trips together. Lying on a sunbed, listening to Take That 'Could it be Magic' and Dina Caroll, 'The Perfect Year' with the sun on my face thinking how lucky we were. We had also met a couple of lovely young men around our age, who we were looking forward to meeting later that day in the hope that between us all we could convince the parents to let us have some sangria. A perfect combination.

My friend's dad had been feeling a bit unwell, but there didn't seem to be any major panic or concerns. Her mum had arranged to get him checked just to be on the safe side with a local doctor. I don't know all the details, and to be honest it was a massive blur (and still is), but hours later that day, it had turned dark and we started to worry that they weren't back. I can't remember the exact time, or how many hours had passed, but I can then remember that my friends mum arrived back alone, something wasn't right. In fact, it couldn't have been any more wrong. I just remember the words leaving her mums mouth, saying that he had died.

Their world changed forever.

I am not going to share the details of what happened then, as it's personal and not my story to share, but I will take you forward to months later when I was lay in my bed worrying that every adult in my life was going to die, and I didn't know when or how. It felt unbearable.

As I already said, I did a fair amount of worrying about everyone else anyway, but now I had hard evidence that I needed to worry, or so I thought. The reality in my world had changed; seriously bad things do happen when we least expect it. That's difficult to get your head around.

When we struggle to understand something, we may then make it our mission to understand or try and control the uncontrollable. I did this through analysis of all the what ifs. I was doing this in secret because I also felt that this was not my trauma, my distress, I was the one that got to come home to my dad, I just needed to get on with it. I now see this differently in a number of ways.

In times of stress or when we have a lot to think about, we can easily find ourselves reverting to our existing habits to help us through.
As I have already talked about my habit, addiction if you like, was to overthinking. I somehow felt that for me to be OK and to manage I had to think everything through. Rather than accepting that what had happened was horrendous and that it would come with a whole host

of feelings, I tried to think my way out of the discomfort.

Thoughts create feelings, more thoughts create more feelings, feelings can build and become more and more intense. We then often look to a behaviour or habit to sooth ourselves, to stop the cycle or avoid the feelings. Yet the feelings are already there, they came with the thoughts.

The behaviours are different for everyone. Drink, drugs, hibernation, doing, cleaning, binge eating, having lots of sex with strangers, isolating ourselves and so on. Now you may look at some of these behaviours and think what's wrong with that, maybe you like drinking or having lots of sex with strangers and that's OK. It's when these habits stop us from living the life we want that we get in our own way and sabotage ourselves.

We can then become almost fixated on the behaviour itself. I will have people come to me and tell me they need to stop doing x, y and z and then all their problems will go away, if only they could stop it.
It's great that people recognise something isn't serving them anymore, and that they want to make a change but we need to go back to the beginning. I don't mean your history and past, I mean where the feelings came from, our thoughts.

"Feeling holds the secret to life and the missing link to connect you to that feeling is thought". The Great Illusion Part 2 Video Series Sydney Banks

It is important for us to listen to the feelings we experience; Sydney Banks described our feelings being like the warning on a computer that there is some kind of virus. It's something for us to listen to, yet we will often try and get rid of them as quickly as possible through the behaviours already mentioned. This will continue the cycle. Let me give you a simple example.

You may have formed a habit that when you feel stressed you go home and have a glass of wine or two. Maybe that's not a big deal.

The thing about habits though is that we can then keep doing this to the point where we don't even realise it's a habit. Before we know it, every time we feel slightly overwhelmed or stressed, we believe we won't settle properly without those glasses of wine as it's worked for us so far. (This is common also with those that believe they struggle socially and feel they can't socialise without a drink).

This isn't true it's a habit that we now have as part of our belief system. Let's just say then that someone decides it's no longer helpful or serving them to drink wine as they feel it gets in their way of other things, they may then start to fixate on stopping the behaviour.

Maybe they will reduce the wine to less per evening. Maybe they will purchase a lower alcohol product. This may work. They may even be able to just stop completely if their belief in their ability is strong enough but what happens when the next really stressful thing happens. They want a solution.

Back to the wine maybe? Replace it with binge eating instead? We often replace it with something else as we see the behaviour, the product or whatever it is as the issue but that's outside in!

Inside out is the way we work. This means that changing any habit begins with the thoughts. Everything I am talking about in this book, and all other aspects of my work.

The more we see about how things work from the inside out, it's like the behaviours just change all on their own without us having to do anything.

Insights…

Seriously awful things happen in life. None of us are going to go through life without experiencing loss. All of us. No amount of wondering, worrying or figuring out will change the outcome of these things. All it actually does is prolong the suffering we experience whilst we think about it time and time again.

This is one of my favourite quotes and helped me through my dad's death,

"It's better to have loved and lost than never to have loved at all". Alfred Lord Tennyson

It's also true for any feelings and not just those of loss. We would never be able to experience the highs without the lows. It goes back to us looking at things from a perspective of being grateful and accepting for what is. I appreciate that this can seem difficult at times. I can remember being so anxious and believing actually that nothing was good, nothing for weeks on end but actually looking back I know that wasn't true.

No matter where we are in life or what is happening, we can always look in this direction. I have worked with people on a number of occasions who at times believe they can't leave the house and this becomes extremely frustrating and sad for them. They would get peace of mind much sooner if they were more accepting of what is.

Deciding that they will make the best out of being in their home as they can, finding joy and contentment within their home. This is possible. Yet often people will resist this, as their thinking is fixated on taking them to a place of disappointment, failure and frustration.

I want to be able to go out. I need it to change and quickly. It is not OK. All of those thoughts create further anxious thinking, more intense feelings and the behaviour as a result of that is likely to be them staying in even more, they may even go to restricting themselves more within their home.

I have heard people say many times that when they have visited third world countries that they have very little, and yet they have smiles on their faces. This was my experience when I stayed in a tribal village in Thailand too. I remember feeling slightly anxious there as I had to sleep on a floor and didn't have access to much food or comfort and yet the families there seemed so happy and content.

They have come to accept what is and they find the joy and love in whatever their situation is.
Now it would be completely naïve to think they are always full of smiles and that they never wander off into a thought place of what if and if only.
This normal and part of being human but it's the holding on to those thoughts, layering thoughts on top of thoughts and believing that we are unable to be happy or content without certain outcomes that creates constant suffering.

I realised through the exploration of these principles, specifically listening to Sydney Banks that I was always looking for happiness and honestly believed at times that it was in a job, in a holiday, a house and lots of other things outside of me.

It was when I started to see that although I had many holidays, moved from a house to a bigger and better house, better cars, more money and so on, that actually I was fully capable and yet never immune from feeling anxious and overwhelmed, and that in those moments none of that stuff actually mattered. I remember at one of the most anxious times I had, thinking to myself, if I actually won one million pounds on the lottery right now, I still couldn't get rid of this feeling.

I really started to see that we get out of our mind what we put in. Sydney Banks talked about it being like putting discs into a computer and although we have moved on a bit since then, the principle is still the same. Take Google for example, it is a fantastic search tool to explore and tell us endless facts. However, the results and outcomes you get out of Google are only as good as what you put into your search.

This makes me laugh as I remember when my daughter first got an iPad and she was learning to spell words. Sat next to me she was typing away, before I had realised I needed to block anything, she put in the words 'lovely granny' and oh my word the site links that popped up were not good!

She also once searched for 'bad daddy' after she had just been cross with her dad that was equally disturbing!

One more thing I want to mention about Google in case I forget. It can be great but it can also be really unhelpful when it comes to anxious thoughts. I remember many times where I would google symptoms and side effects to tablets. It never ended well. If you think about who is going to take the time to go on a forum and discuss symptoms?

Probably not someone who is out enjoying their life. It's not a fair or balanced view. It's a view of a community of people who are also struggling. I eventually banned myself from Google at times of stress. It helped a lot.

Back to the point. If I link it back to anxiety, I was waking up each morning and my search in my head went something like this…. Am I anxious today? Am I having any physical symptoms?

It was like a habitual scan of my mind and body to search for the dreaded anxiety. You probably know what I am going to say next, in that low and behold, before long, there was the churning stomach and the tingling hands.

There comes the virus detector I mentioned earlier. The feelings, warning me or telling me something. In this case that I had a whole load of anxious thinking and worry going on.

How do we stop this then? By understanding its thought, an illusion I was creating in my mind. I then started to realise through this exploration that a completely different perspective and choice of thoughts was always just at my fingertips, minutes or even seconds away.

As sad as that felt at that time, it was also quite freeing to realise. It meant in some ways I didn't need to keep bettering my outside world. I could start to see it as enough; it had always been enough. I realised I just hadn't been listening to what I knew inside as I was too busy thinking my way through every problem I could get my hands on. I also realised that this would never come to an end. The gift of thought is wonderful in its nature that we have constant access to it, creating often wonderful experiences yet it is also accessible endlessly when we are worrying.

When we are looking to solve a problem in our minds it's like we are trying to clear the mind yet what we are doing is actually creating more things to consider, we are contaminating the mind more and more. I now see and have experienced that behind that contamination is a much more peaceful mind.

As I have talked about loss and grief in this chapter I wanted to share that even in death this new understanding has brought me insights. I wasn't in this place when I lost my dad, or my friend lost her dad and so I was riddled with fear, anxiety and the deepest sadness. Now of course they are all part of the full range of feelings and experiences we may have in grief. But I now also see there are more.

Sadly, I lost my uncle this year. He was far too young to die. He had been an amazing male role model in my life as a child. He would come and see us most Saturdays for years on end, bring us a 10p mix of sweets and take us to the park. I was desperately sad, angry and confused about his death. Yet there was something different in this experience of grief. I seemed much more able to also feel grateful in his death. Grateful for being able to have had him in my life and for the time spent with him. Now this may seem obvious but actually in grief before I haven't experienced this in the same way.

I have spent much of my grief in the past lost in thought. Thoughts about how I would manage or cope, thoughts about how death would face all of us and so much more. I hadn't experienced warmth or love in death. I have now. I was able to see that even in the saddest of times; we can experience a warm feeling of love if we allow ourselves to.

I could feel deep sadness and loss one minute and then a deep gratitude the next. I accepted all of it. I didn't question it. We think our way through life. Thought is a gift. Wherever you are in any given moment is all you can give away. This is where taking care of US is important.

I also realised in recent years that I could have held on to experiences that happened all my life, holding it against other people, like my dad for his shit choices, but I was actually holding it against myself. Without forgiveness I may have felt anger and frustration and this would have controlled so many aspects of my life.

"Forgive others, not because they deserve forgiveness, but because you deserve peace". Jonathan Lockwood Huie

I share this quote for anyone that may be reading what I am saying and thinking that there is no way they could forgive what someone has done to them. I could forgive my dad for some of the decisions he made because I see compassionately that at the time, he did the best he could with what he knew.

I appreciate that not everybody's experience seems as straight forward as mine, so I wanted to share this as it's for you, not for them.

I also just want to say that I don't have this all figured out because again part of being human means will can easily fall back into our thinking, taking us away from the feeling of peace and love.

I can still listen to certain songs now and feel instantly sad and upset about my dad's passing even after ten years. This is also OK. I allow it. I accept it and I continue living alongside all of it.

CHAPTER 10

It is what it is?

I used to find this phrase so irritating and now I find myself living by it. If someone would say it is what it is my head would instantly go to a place I've mentioned before that usually starts with the word 'yes but'.

There is an even quicker way that I now access this state of mind, which I initially heard from Michael Neill.

Full Stop.

When we are in school, we are encouraged to be creative and expand the words we use. Tell a story. Using adjectives, describe and elaborate and make our words tell a much more interesting and encapsulating story. I was pretty good at English, no wonder, as an over thinker I could always add to my words.

It was almost frowned upon if you used limited words and ended abruptly with a full stop. Now this may have got me some great grades in English classes but it was creating havoc in my personal life. I needed to learn to use my full stop more frequently and quicker. Michael Neill helped me to see this.

Let me explain a bit more about what I mean.

Say you have had a fall out with a friend. Maybe they have said something hurtful to you. This would be a whole open forum for me in my mind to figure it all out. Why? How dare they? Was I wrong? Were they wrong? Who is on my side? How do I get out of this situation? Where does this end? What do I need?

And this could develop into hours of exploration in my head. Then I may speak to another friend to go over it all again.

This was pointless and only kept the anxious thoughts going and going.

It is only ever our perspective, it's OK to feel the way we feel but it's also OK for others to feel how they feel too. All we are doing by attempting to convince others or work out why they think the way they think is continuing our suffering. The minute we compare ourselves to others we are creating suffering.

I can't remember who I once heard say this but it hit home with me,

It's none of our business what others think of us.

Sounds a bit harsh but it really isn't our business. Now obviously there is a line and actually if people are outwardly aggressive and unkind this is not OK, but our job is to take ourselves away from this treatment, to see it's not about us and it's definitely not our job to figure the other person out and ask all the whys. This will not get you anywhere other than completely lost in thought.

This understanding that I have talked about all the way through this book is not an intellectual understanding, it doesn't matter how clever you are, what your life is like – we all have access to that same guide in life that I have mentioned, your internal sat nav.

Whether you are new to these ideas, or you have already explored previously, it's likely that at some point you will find yourself saying 'I'm not getting it.'

The only thing in your way is you. However, its important you don't beat yourself up for that, and realise that the insights are always there for the taking. They often crop up when we least expect them, as I've already said and the more frustrated we become about 'not getting it', the more distracted our minds become and the less likely we are to see anything new.

One of my favourite phrases when I was trying to use my full stop more was 'so what'. Now you will come up with or find yourself using your own phrases and the words are actually not important, it's the sentiment behind what we are saying to ourselves.

Depending on my state of mind at the time I would need to use the words 'so what' many times before something clicked and I realised what I was doing and that I was getting lost in the 'ifs' and 'buts' again.

Over time this became easier. The more I saw in these principles, the easier it was to listen to my wisdom and gut that would regularly tell me so what. Just stick with it. It is what it is.

CHAPTER 11

Love

One thing I did notice in the early days of my anxiety was that when I was laughing, experiencing joy or more specifically love, I wasn't anxious. It was as though it was impossible for me to be anxious when I was experiencing love, almost basking in it.

I now see that I am at my most content when happy looking towards the core of what we all are, love. When I start to feel overwhelmed or unsettled, I now see that I am taking myself away from love. I am thinking myself away from it. I am now also able to see that rather than being rid of anxiety, I am always in those more challenging moments, aiming to get closer to the love.

Now I don't mean this in terms of love like we may describe as being in love with someone, loving friends or family, I mean the type of love and contentment that is everywhere.

The sky, the birds, the fresh air, my favourite chocolate, a comfy sofa. Now as I have said all the way through this book everything is inside out and so I know that the sofa, the chocolate and the sky for example cannot make me feel love, but my perception of whatever I am experiencing in any moment, being present in that moment takes me back towards the love. This can be in its simplest form. Just content and seeing love in 'what is' no matter how big or small.

When we think about contentment and being happy, we can often look towards 'things' outside of us to make us happy. If I can just find x, if I could afford y and so on. Yet true happiness, and that feeling of love, doesn't come from these things, we all have access to love no matter where we are in life. It's at the core of all of us.

Looking back towards LOVE

L - Listen. I mean listen to yourself and others. Now you may feel that you do listen well already. I always saw myself as a good listener, I had even had training on it in the workplace but I now see I wasn't truly listening. Take an argument for example. You may be having a disagreement with your partner. You are sat having a heated discussion, attempting to understand more about what is going on so that you can get past the discomfort.

If you are listening but actually in that listening you are already thinking about your next statement and linking it back to you, then you are really not listening. We are only listening when we have no pre conceived ideas or agenda in the conversation. This is why often arguments go round in circles because you will not see your partner in a different or more compassionate light if you are not open to hearing anything you don't already think you know.

This applies to yourself and listening to yourself. Are you actually paying attention to your virus detector? If you are saying things along the lines of, I am always, I know what I am like. What happens next is, and anything that implies you already know, it won't be helpful. Listen as if you know nothing and then you will see more than you ever thought possible.

O – Observe. This is really about us observing our lives, and the world around us, with the ability to take a step back from our existing thoughts about something. It links in with listening. If we think about helping others with anxiety, this is where being alongside them, rather than fixing, is more beneficial. When we are overwhelmed it can be so easy to jump into our stress head first. We have a sense of urgency, a panic. This again is where it can be helpful to slow your mind by becoming the observer in what is happening. Observers see much more than those in the thick of it.

V - Validate your progress. I hear daily, many many times, people judging and criticising themselves for what they have done. It appears it's much easier to see what you haven't achieved rather than actually how far you have come. Any progress, no matter how small, is progress. We need to validate and acknowledge all the steps, no matter how small we see them. Again, the size of the achievements is still only our perceptions so rather than judge them, acknowledge and validate them.

Some days doing the bare minimum is more than enough, and is actually an achievement. We always have other choices and just because we only got dressed and put one wash on today doesn't mean we have failed. We could have stayed in bed.

E - Embrace the journey. I appreciate that this can often be difficult to see. Why would we want to embrace a journey that feels difficult? Well I can honestly say that as time goes by and I came out the other side of some quite challenging times, I see that there was something in all of it for me.

I can look back and see that it has brought me to where I am now. If you are not there yet that's also OK. This is what I have already mentioned when talking about our full stop or so what. It is what is and although at times we would rather be anywhere else than where we are, it will always change, the more we accept where we are, the easier it becomes.

Let me give you a little example of where this was helpful for me.

I remember a time when my daughter was off school ill. I needed her in. I was busy and overwhelmed. I had loads to do. I was also worried about her as she has asthma and when she's unwell it can settle quickly on her chest and I feel helpless. I don't like the idea of her feeling breathless. It scares me.

We were in my bedroom with the tv on and I was sat by her just going over all of this stuff in my mind. For a minute the drums must have stopped and I heard the flute. (The more you explore this stuff, the easier this will become for you too). I realised in a split second what I was doing. I was frustrated with what was and I had absolutely no control over it. I gave in. I decided everything could wait. I decided I could lie with her and watch tv and that I could also do this without worrying about her chest and all the stuff I haven't done.

We had a lovely afternoon. We laughed, we cuddled and we both really enjoyed ourselves. This was not how the day started. We always have the option to change our experience of anything, through our thoughts. We deserve this. We are all equally able to access this peace of mind no matter what the situation.

I used my full stop.

I hope you continue to explore and see this more and more for yourself.

I want you to remember a few things...

This little section is simply a brief reminder, a page you can look back on if you feel you need it. Maybe your mood is low, your awareness has shifted, and you are not thinking as clearly, maybe believing every thought you have...

Remember...

Your innate wellbeing is always there, underneath the noise. Listen out for the flute!

The physical symptoms are harmless, they are a response to your thoughts and so don't need to be feared (I know, I know they feel shit but honestly, they are OK)

All of this is transient and will pass – always.

Acceptance of how and who you are in any moment, will allow the feelings to pass much quicker.

Everything is inside out.

You are currently experiencing your thoughts. Living in the feeling of them right now.

Thoughts are neutral until we bring them to life.

You are NOT broken.

You are OK

Honestly you really are!

I wanted to share a simple extract from The Cherry Log Sermons by the Reverend Fred Craddock. I originally came across this in Creating The Impossible by Michael Neill.

Here is an unlikely conversation between a man and a greyhound dog.

I said to the dog, "Are you still racing?'

'No,' the dog replied.

"Well, what was the matter? Did you get too old to race?'

'No, I still had some race in me.'

'Well, what then? Did you not win?'

'I won over a million dollars for my owner.'

'Well, what was it? Bad treatment?'

'Oh, no,' the dog said. 'They treated us royally when we were racing.'

'Did you get crippled?'

'No.'

'Then why?' I pressed. 'Why?'

The dog answered, 'I quit.'

'You quit?'

'Yes,' he said. 'I quit.'

'Why did you quit?'

'I just quit because after all that running and running and running, I found out that the rabbit I was chasing wasn't even real.'

Followed by some words of wisdom by Michael Neill.

'The future is like this too. Not only is it unpredictable, but there's actually no such thing as the future to begin with. The whole idea is made up in our own mind'.

If you want to explore further and there are loads of coaches, books, videos and so on to continue to explore. I would recommend that anyone goes back to the original source and watch Sydney Banks lectures that are available online. This is always a great place to start.

If you would like to explore specifically with me, I would love to hear from you. You can access me through my website www.sarietaylor.com or via any of my social media accounts @sarietaylorcoaching

Thank you so much for believing in me enough to get this far in my book and I hope this book has at the very least made you curious to learn and see more.

All my Love Sarie

THE END
(Or maybe it's actually just the beginning?

HOPE (These snippets of hope have remained untouched by me).

"Just wanted to give you a little update on xxxxx. Just got back from our local McDonald's with her and my youngest two, absolutely un heard of for her some time back. Too close to home, too worried if she seen anyone from school (or ANYONE in general) she said no at first then said " ok, I'll come actually" I've just asked her how she was there she said " meh" I said " well I'm glad you came , because we really enjoyed you being there . And that was it...
She just looks altogether fresher, smiley, happy, chatty. She still comes home for lunch, and still HATES school, and if she goes off on a little rant will say how much she hates it, struggles etc, a lot is just typical, teenage negativity , hating school " normal " stuff. But I can see in her behaviour she's struggling less...AND she's got her self a little Saturday job at a cafe, she's wanted to work since she was like 5! She's money mad she used to get upset and say things like "how will I ever get a job when I can't even speak to people" and here she is.. shouting table, orders out ect... It does help it's a little old people's cafe but will build that confidence.

I wish I could say she goes running through school without a care in the world but I know it doesn't work like that, and I'm happy (even of she doesn't want to admit it! That shes coping, she making it through the day, shes doing more now than she would have ever dreamt, only this time last year. She's even started watching your videos (with a little bribery) I think even subconsciously, something is going in!

I can't imagine it's anything else but your help. I myself couldn't have imagined what a changed girl she'd be now from last year. THANK YOU so much. She's not %100 "fixed" but baby steps, and maturity, and once shes fully ready to take it all onboard, she's going to be set for life with the tools you've given her.
Keep doing what you're doing, you're amazing, I see you always go above and beyond. It matters to you, and it is helping people like me help out children and see that little light back behind their eyes.
Wanted you to know how much you've helped us xx"

"Hi Sarie. I hope all is well. I love watching your blogs, I can't believe how much they have helped me and I didn't even realise I needed help. Xxxxx has gone to Uni and I couldn't believe it when she "casually" told me that she'd spent all night in A&E with a friend who had hurt her knee.... I would have never have thought that she would have been able to do that - AMAZING, all thanks to you "

"Hi Sarie, I just wanted to share with you that last night I went to a Michelin star restaurant and survived! I may have had a melt down about an hour before leaving, telling my husband there was no way I could do it and may have downed a glass of wine when I got there but I did it! I had 2 courses, no panic attacks or dramas and would even go as far as to say I actually enjoyed it.

Not many people will understand just how much of a big deal this is but if you'd have asked me 2 years ago, going to a Michelin star restaurant would have been my absolute worst nightmare. As you know I used to be petrified of going out to eat anywhere, worst of all somewhere posh.

I used to have episodes where I was so anxious and felt so awful I just couldn't eat anything at all.
I have seen three different counsellors over the years for the problem as the phobia has significantly affected my life to the point where I'd be anxious weeks in advance of something in the diary, making myself feel constantly ill. My husband has always wanted to go to a Michelin star restaurant so when his parents said they'd like to treat him for his birthday he was over the moon.

I never intended to go with them but since doing your course Sarie and following you on Facebook I have gone from strength to strength and somehow found the confidence to say yes to last night. My husband was so thrilled and pleased to have me there I don't think he could quite believe it. Just wanted to say a huge thank you for helping me to achieve something I never thought would have been possible. x"

"I was in a very dark place over 2 years ago and thought there was no light at the end of the tunnel. Everyday was filled with anxiety, panic attacks and very negative Intrusive thoughts. Really thought my life was over !! Then I can across this amazing lady who at first I thought there's no way this works !! I couldn't take pills as was so sensitive to chemicals and the fact that I thought I would choke on them !! I watched her lives ,podcasts joined some of her online sessions and read all about the three principles . It's not an easy journey but once it all clicks that actually don't fight the thoughts just let them come and go ,it falls into place. I'm now doing things that back in the day I actually didn't think I would be here to do !! Please stick with Sarie for she really will help you see the light and help you understand about the three principles. I still have the odd off day ,who doesn't but it's how I deal with them now that makes all the difference."

"I have recently purchased the manual and joined the members club. What a difference this has made, it's not perfect but it's a million times better than before. I cannot recommend Sarie enough for the straight forward no nonsense advice. My daughter and myself have come on leaps and bounds. I understand better what she is going through, I will never completely understand, but that's ok. My daughter understands that she is ok. She loves the taxi analogy and uses that every morning. To the point now she gets up herself makes breakfast for us all and is happy on a good day, which now far out way the bad. Huge thanks Sarie xx"

"I did the one week anxiety course with Sarie and it was really informative. Sarie replied to my emails daily which was fab and continued to do so even after the week had ended which was so kind of her when I was in a difficult place. Sarie posts free things all the time on FB which is amazing as she gives up her own time to do so. Thank you Sarie . I would recommend the one week anxiety course for anyone suffering with any sort of anxiety as the techniques and information is widely applicable."

"Hi Sarie,
I just wanted to say I have nearly completed your booklet and something has really resonated with me (well actually there are quite a lot of things).
When you were discussing about it's ok to be average it made me examine my own beliefs about this as instantly my initial response was no it is better to always achieve the best you can rather than be average. When I have been examining this it takes me back to my childhood in a working class area in which finances were tight for my family and my father in particular had very working class male values of women staying at home (which despite my mum having an aspiration to open an hairdressing business was dismissed by my dad which she always regretted not doing).

Therefore I created a belief from a young age that my passport out of the same situation that my mum was in was through Education and to succeed and always be independent. I went on to get 2 degrees and an MA and other diplomas in various things and a successful career.

However, this belief has always created anxiety by having too high expectations in that I always have to achieve and succeed in many areas of my life not just education which can often lead to rigidity with no fun or spontaneity!!
So reading and hearing you on the tape saying it is ok to be average has made me really challenge this belief and really resonated with me. As I have become aware that

this belief filters through into having too high expectations of myself but more importantly my children and partner and I always have to keep checking myself so I don't hold unrealistic and too high expectations of my family. (Whilst it is good to hold some expectations I know before now I have been disappointed if my expectations have not been met which isn't fair on my family!). Therefore, it was lovely reading the sentence to strive more to be average! This is something that I now want to add to my thinking. It will be my new mantra - It is ok to be average!! Just even saying it out load to myself takes the ball and chains I have been carrying around with me and I feel lighter.

I also connected with the escalator and the five floors and it is so true depending on which floor you are on dictates your responses and subsequent behaviours.

I would just like to say a heartfelt thankyou as I had lightbulb moment when reading that section of the book. I also know that my own children and partner will benefit from me having read this booklet and listened to the videos."

"Just wanted to feedback - I acquired a fear of flying about 10 years ago that showed itself physically weeks before any flight but more severely a couple of days before - right up to getting on the flight. Great for weight loss but I felt dreadful! Many times I didn't think

I'd make it on the flight. I was ready to change jobs to avoid the one flight I have to do each year. I even had a saying as I crossed the aeroplane doorway, "goodbye beautiful world" - very dramatic! I'd totally bought into my stories! Anyhow, after following you and reading your manual - I've just been on 4 flights in 2 weeks - 2 of which were transatlantic. No drama, no worry, no physical symptoms, no actual dialogue - only the factual, e.g. have I got the passports... still! So thank you! Your work works! I know you know - but just wanted to feedback! "

"Hi Sarie, I just wanted to share an experience I had today.

I was at a training event this evening for work and whilst sitting happily in my seat listening to the presentation I turned my head and thought I got a wave of slight dizziness.

In a split second my brain had fired off a hundred thoughts 'maybe it's my heart arrhythmia, maybe I'm going to keel over, oh no don't get anxious, that will make it worse, I've got indigestion, maybe its chest pain, I've got sweaty palms, I feel sick, maybe my dental abscess is making me ill, maybe it's the antibiotics, what if I throw up, I need to get out of here, ahhh!'

And then I stopped and took a deep breath and realised all my symptoms were anxiety related and recognised that I'd just triggered a spiral of very unhelpful thoughts.

Even though I felt awful for a few minutes as my body reset itself, I was able to look at from the inside out and by telling myself it will pass, I will be ok, and almost smiling to myself because I knew I'd completely made myself feel like that, within 5mins it had passed and I felt absolutely fine again.
None of those thoughts were true. It's amazing how quickly we can induce intense feelings and symptoms but also reassuring how quickly we can reset if we leave the thinking alone. I would not have responded this way before knowing about the 3 principles. They rock! X"

Printed in Great Britain
by Amazon